FEEL GREAT

ATTRACT

GREATNESS

You Have What it Takes

DEREK BONIFACE

 FriesenPress

Suite 300 - 990 Fort St
Victoria, BC, V8V 3K2
Canada

www.friesenpress.com

Copyright © 2020 by Derek Boniface
First Edition — 2020

All rights reserved.

ISBN
978-1-5255-8316-2 (Hardcover)
978-1-5255-8317-9 (Paperback)
978-1-5255-8318-6 (eBook)

1. SELF-HELP, PERSONAL GROWTH, HAPPINESS

Distributed to the trade by The Ingram Book Company

TABLE OF CONTENTS

PREFACE

Why this book?

We are what we attract, so why don't we be the absolute best possible versions of ourselves? There are many answers to this question, such as fear of failure, I can never achieve something big, I don't have the skill set. But what if I told you that life becomes easier, more enjoyable, and more exciting when you really go for your dreams? And when I say dreams, I'm not talking about what you think you deserve or think you can get, I'm saying, what does your perfect life really look like? What I have learned and experienced in life is that if you make a decision, and truly decide to commit to live your dream to its fullest, you will learn more about yourself than you have ever learned before, which will help you make your dreams a reality. Anything that you have ever desired is waiting to be born through you. It's your destiny to put life into your desires. The one big problem with this is we all have self-limiting beliefs holding us back. In this book, I will take you on a journey, releasing your self-limiting beliefs and creating new, more empowering beliefs. This will help you feel better than you currently feel and bring you to a feeling that will help you attract what you really want in life, because whatever we feel, we will attract more of that feeling.

Should our goal then be to feel the best we have ever felt, the most often? I have yet to think of something that I want more than to feel AMAZING all the time. I think of my relationship with my wife and kids and that feeling brings me to the feeling of love and gratitude. When you feel pure love, pure gratitude, and pure abundance, there really is no better feeling. What more can you want? When you can get to a point where you need nothing because you feel like you have everything, that is the moment that your life will change. Everything that you have ever wanted in life is ready to be born through you. Your job is to become your potential and release your dreams into the world.

That's easier said than done for most of us, as there is a serious issue in society today, with so much noise. People live busy lives, with school, work, kids, projects, relationships, sports . . . When do you have time for yourself? Not to mention with debt rising, the divorce rate increasing, obesity becoming an epidemic, to-do lists longer than a spoiled kid's Christmas list. It seems like more and more people are waking up with cancer, and people living sedentary lifestyles, feeling like shit or worrying about tomorrow. These are all real problems, and without the right mindset, it's only going to get worse. The good news is I have found the power from within and you also contain the same unlimited power to live a life with unlimited success and happiness. No matter where you are in life, what your situation is, how much debt you are in, how much stress you may have, how much physical or emotional pain you may have, your dreams are waiting for you to bring them to life. If life has beaten you up and you've hit rock bottom, you can feel better. Even if you're living a great life, you can still feel better. You can wake up with more excitement, you can have more energy, you can feel more love and abundance and you can live the life of your dreams with a sense of knowing, you deserve it! There is a power from within that I want you to tap into, and with the chapters in the book, it will help you feel and understand what it takes to feel great and to attract greatness. I believe this book will help unlock your brain to achieve anything you desire. It will give you the excitement you once had for life, like when you were a child waking up on Christmas day. This book will give you the confidence and courage to live a life you may have never realized you could ever have. More importantly, this book will make you feel good, and when you feel good, your life will start to change. So get ready to start feeling better, get ready to live a life of hope, a life of purpose, a life that when you wake up, you are waking up with a feeling of excitement and appreciation, instead of "Ugh, I have to work today." Are you ready to live the life of your dreams? Are you ready to learn more about yourself than you have ever learned before? Are you ready to experience the freedom and joy that life has to offer? If so, let's go . . .

Who am I?

I am just a normal guy, a husband to a beautiful wife (Carrie), a father to two healthy, cute kids (Cali and Beau), a twin brother to a guy who is also my best bud (Jeff), a son to two amazing loving parents; I am also a leader, a friend, and the creator of everything I desire.

I have discovered my purpose, and I have felt what it feels like to achieve what most of us strive for. I have felt complete self-awareness, I have felt the power from within to heal all and create all that is good in our life. I have understood how to tap into this source to allow the pure energy flow through our bodies, to help us understand our potential.

I am composed of everything you are, but I can say, with confidence, "I am free, and I feel great." I expect greatness. I live life with a glass half full attitude. I am living a great life. I have a great career in the health industry, my health is on point, I have a beautiful family, a dream home, and my bank account is growing by the day. Everything I have ever wanted, I have found a way to attract in my life. I say this by no means to brag, but to give you hope that you can find what you're looking for, as life was not always like this for me. It took a big problem for me to figure this out, as I have lived in debt, I have lived with chronic pain, I was drinking too much, I was waking up every day feeling blah and living each day like it was Groundhog Day. It took the biggest struggle of my life to really dig deep and understand the power. But, the bigger the struggle, the bigger the reward.

With over 14 years of immersing myself in self-development and removing layers of bad habits and bad thoughts that were holding me back from realizing my potential, I have finally figured out what all these books are talking about. I cannot wait to share this power to help you achieve whatever it is you desire.

I am a person that you can most likely relate to, as I have been through it all; but I am also a person who has done the work to achieve the feeling of joy, abundance, confidence, success, freedom, and appreciation on a daily basis. So I urge you to use my leg work, stories, and tips to fast track your life to instantly make a change for the better.

Whether you are looking to improve your health, improve your wealth, improve your relationships, or just plain, live stress free and filled with love and gratitude, this book is for you.

INTRODUCTION

Before you dive into the rich knowledge that I am about to share, I want to express my most sincere gratitude for picking up this book and giving it a read. I truly believe that the more people who can discover how to reach their potential, the more the world will be a better place for all.

To get the most out of this book, I want you to understand a few things. First, we are in the perfect place at the perfect time. No matter how good or how bad our situation is, there is no better place than right now. You're either at a place where life is feeling absolutely amazing and powerful or you're at a point where right now is the time where you are going to get the information you need to make a decision to change your life.

Second, I want you to understand two laws: the Law of Attraction and the Law of Emergence. The Law of Attraction states that like attracts like. Whoever you are and whatever you think about most, that is what you will attract into your life. Thoughts then become things.

The Law of Emergence is a principle that talks about you having everything you ever wanted. Everything that you want already exists in you. Your desires are being born inside you and trying to release themselves into the world.

I want you to understand that by using these two laws, you can be, do, or have anything you want in life. That said, people make many mistakes along the way with using these laws and therefore start attracting the exact opposite of what they think they are trying to attract. This is why you see people becoming broke when they really want to be rich and they can't figure out why.

In this book, I want to share with you my journey of learning about these laws and going through the mistakes I made to bring myself to a better place of understanding, and how I used these laws to help me live the life of my dreams.

It will take having an open mind, it will take releasing old thought patterns, it will take learning how to surrender to your pure self, and it will take work, but what I promise you is that this journey is an exciting journey. It's a journey that will help you tap into your great self, and the work will become effortless. So get ready to go to work on yourself, to unleash the desires that are waiting to be born.

Take care of yourself first;
you can only give what you have

You are the most important person. You are always the most important person you can take care of. No one else is going to take care of you, or even understand what exactly you need to feel better. If there is anything I want you to take from this book, it's to take care of yourself first. Be selfish!! Good, you're done now . . . Thanks for picking up my book.

All jokes aside, let's take a look at the average Joe's life. Wake up, say, "Ugh, it's Monday," have a shower, get breakfast, go to work, hate my job, wish I was somewhere else, come home, eat supper, veg on the couch, watch some TV, and go to bed. Rinse, wash, repeat. Throw kids into the mix, a possible commute to your work, maybe you're out of shape, lacking energy, and you haven't had anything good happen in a while, you're probably used to feeling crappy as you don't know any better or at least cannot remember how good you once felt. The reality is, this is what many people's lives are like: they do what they need to do to survive, instead of doing what they need to do to thrive.

Over the past 14 years working in the health industry, I have come across many mothers, and they all say, "I want to lose my baby weight." I then ask them how old their baby is, and often I get answers like, 14, 15, 16, and "They have moved out now." I get it, life is busy, especially for mothers, as they seem to care the most, but to not find time to work on yourself could be the greatest tragedy of all time. Remember, you can only give what you have, and as much as you are giving, giving, giving, soon you will come to a point where you have nothing left to give at all.

The good news is that all this can change, and it can change quickly, as you do not need to learn anything new to attract what you want into your life—you already have all the answers. You are already great, you are abundant, you are healthy, you are pure love. You just might not remember that you are, because, over time, you have developed some thoughts or beliefs that have been blocking your potential and stopping you from realizing your powers from within. Throughout this book, there are going to be questions, routines, suggestions, and ideas that will help you to break the patterns of your old thoughts and allow you to realize how great you are. All I can ask you to do is to pick a couple that resonate with you and roll with them. Do what feels right for you or what you can see yourself enjoying. We are all on our own journey, and there is no right way. It HAS to be your way. With that said, thank you for exploring your potential, and get ready to feel the power within to make you feel 10 feet tall and bulletproof.

CHAPTER 1

GOAL/DREAM BIG

As we embark the journey of this book and as we talk about dreaming big and setting goals, know that anything is possible. Napolean Hill said, "Whatever you believe and you can bring your mind to conceive, you can achieve". Albert Einstein says that your intelligence is determined not by your IQ, but your ability to stay focused on your goal. Your imagination is more powerful than knowledge. With knowing this, I want you to have an open mind and really expand your thoughts to as big as you can imagine. The only limitations we have, are the ones we set on ourselves. So as you read this, imagine that you have all the money and all the power in the world, what would you be doing?

What do I want you to get out of this chapter?

I want you to understand that your brain is always working, but if you do not have a destination, your brain will bring you places you probably do not want to go. There is serious power in creating an image of what you want in life and who you want to become. The crazy part is, your dream self (whoever that looks like) already lives inside you. Your job is to bring this part of you to life, by removing self-limiting thoughts and beliefs, and by creating new beliefs and thoughts. By the end of this chapter, I want you to think of a big desire that you have, and know that what a desire really is, is a part of you trying to emerge, to become a reality. Once you are able to release this beast from within, not only will you become who you want to become, but you will get what you have always wanted. So the first step in getting what you want is to find what you desire and be laser focused.

Here is my story to understanding goals

It was just after I finished university (Brock) when I decided to take control of my life (in the summer of 2006). I picked up a book by Brian Tracey, entitled, *Goals*. The book came with a DVD and a workbook. After watching the DVD first, I realized the power of goal setting. I then decided to write down 10 goals on a white sheet of paper. Believe it or not, this is the first time I had ever written down a goal, or at least consciously remembering writing one down. A couple years passed and I was cleaning up my basement and I found my goal sheet. I took a look, and I was able to cross off all 10 items. It was at this moment I realized the potential of writing down a goal.

Unfortunately, all my goals were either how much money I wanted to make or materialistic in some way. Yes, it's good to have things in your life, but things do not bring you happiness. Test this for yourself. Can you think of a time where you really wanted something (let's say a new car), and you purchased it. Yes, you would have felt great, but fast forward a couple of years, do you still feel the excitement of having the car? There are studies that show that over time, our happiness fades for things, like buying some new clothes, getting into the school you wanted, buying that new house; happiness always fades when something is not new anymore. This can be a scary trap that some people fall into, because a way for people to feel awesome is to keep buying new stuff (I fell into this trap), as this can be a fast way to live a life in debt or chasing happiness through things, which is quite the opposite to setting goals on becoming who you want to become. So this is a question I am posing to you, Who do you want to become? What feelings do you want to share more with the world?

The power of setting a goal

Having a goal is exciting; it feels purposeful, motivating; it feels like you're on a mission, which ultimately makes you feel good. Have you ever heard a story or known somebody who has retired from work and they become lifeless? Many times, in my opinion, this is because they don't see purpose; they are not trying to achieve anything.

The reality is, many people do not set goals; in other words, they do not know what they want. I actually think this is a huge problem. Think about it. If you don't know what you want, your brain is just going at random and will search for instant gratification, which often leads to temptation. Just think, if you were to live years of your life just grabbing the things you wanted, how much trouble would your life be in?

I ask myself, why would a reasonable, rational person not set a goal? A couple of answers come to mind. Setting a goal can be fearful. Fear of failure can set in. Lack of belief in oneself to reach the goal, or maybe they think of a goal and realize how much work it will take to achieve the goal and that scares them off. I have witnessed many times in my life, that people do not like to set goals because they are in a habit of never reaching them. At the same time they realize all the work and the change that is required to accomplish their goal and they get scared. Not only have I witnessed this over and over again in others, I have also experienced this in myself. The easiest thing to do is to give up, but the hardest thing to do is to keep going. It's easy to smile when things are good, but what about when things get tough? Everyone says they want to be a beast, until they realize what beasts really do. Beasts wake up early, and go down later. They hunt for what they want and they keep going, day in and day out, there is no rest.

To realize that you are anything but average and that a beast lies within all of us, may be the moment where you realize that life is limitless and abundant. Many people have come before you with less and have achieved more. There are so many people that will live life without even living it. Whatever you desire is your choice; I am merely saying that when you figure out your purpose and realize how powerful you are, life becomes exciting, and waking up early and doing your daily exercise becomes easy. It comes from a place of wanting instead of needing to do the work.

What else do I need to know about goal setting?

Accomplishing a goal often takes change, and finding the time to want to change is the hard part. That is why you hear a lot of people waiting until the last possible moment to make the decision to change. I recently read a meme from the meme master himself Jeff Boniface (my brother), which said, "I don't' procrastinate, I intentionally wait until the last minute because then I will be older, and therefore wiser." Check out his Instagram for non stop memes, but on a serious note, please read on. Most people make a change when it's coming to a point in their life where they are sick and tired of being sick and tired. When this point happens, and you make a decision, that is when the ball of momentum will shift. Dr. Joe Dispenza (a world renown doctor who studies the brain) has a message that talks about making a change when things are good in your life. Why wait until things are tough? Making a change is hard enough as is; can you imagine making a change when there is added stress weighing you down?

If nothing changes, you will get what you've always gotten.

What I want to help you with is to give you the courage to have an understanding about why it's important for you to set goals now, and to set goals that match what you desire.

First off, you're one step ahead if you can think of a goal worth striving for. I want to challenge you to set a goal so big that it gets you excited. It should be something that you have always wanted, but maybe you have been too scared to dream or have believed that you could never achieve. I dare you to set this goal, as here is what is going to happen once you do. You will wake up with more excitement and you will stretch your limits to realize your potential. The bigger the goal, the more you will discover your potential inside.

Has this ever happened to you, you wake up really early throughout the week, and yet it is so hard to wake up and, come the weekend, your chance to sleep in, you wake up even earlier and with more excitement? It happens to the best of us; it's because you are excited to do what you want to do with your day. Here is the thing, you can feel like this every day. I am living it, as many other successful leaders are. It's a choice of what we chose to focus on, and by thinking of your goal first thing in the morning, it should help you feel like you are waking up with purpose.

Begin by writing down a goal on a piece of paper. Feel free to even throw out the piece of paper after you write on it, as there is something magical about writing it down. There are 10,000 connections between your hand and your brain. By writing things down, you are creating or deepening your neural pathways. If you were to type out your goals on a computer, or text yourself a note, there are only 3000 connections from your fingers to your brain and you would not deepen the neural pathways as much as you would from writing your ideas or goals down on paper. The deeper the neural pathways, the easier it will be for you to create the habits needed to attract what it is you really want. Picture a rain forest with trees and grass everywhere. Picture an elephant going through a forest and making a new path through the trees and high grass. Once this pathway is started, more and more wildlife will use the path, as it gets easier to travel in the rough terrain. Creating deep neural pathways makes it easier on yourself to get into the habits needed to create the life of your dreams. By writing your goals down with ink and paper, and creating those neural pathways to attract new thoughts will allow the pathways to deepen, which will help build new connections to allow more ideas and thoughts to help you towards your goal.

So how does all this work?

Your brain is a goal-striving machine. A good book for you to read is *Psycho-Cybernetics* by Maxwell Maltz, as this book helps explain the workings of the mind.

If you give your brain a goal, your brain has to go to work on achieving this goal; this is the way we are wired.

There will be some tips coming, but first I just want you to now think of something that you really want. The bigger the goal, the better. Just think, if the goal is to make an extra $100 dollars, this probably will not help you wake up with excitement, compared to if you had a goal of making one million dollars; this might—at least it would get me waking up excited.

What I don't want you to worry about is the HOW. When you think about the how, it's a form of disbelief. I will talk about this in a later chapter. You might be thinking then, Well, how am I going to make the million dollars? Trust me when I say, if you have a goal written down and you are visualizing what it is like to have a million dollars, an idea will come, maybe not at that moment, that day, or that week, but an idea will come sooner than later. You will just need to allow that thought to come into your mind to feel what its like to achieve your desire. In fact, once you have the feeling when you think of your goal, it's not even necessary to think about your goal any more as long as you can harness the feeling in the first place. Your feelings will act like a magnet and bring more of those feelings into your life. The Laws of Attraction states that whatever you feel, more of those feelings will come rushing into existence as like attracts like.

At this stage, just write down a goal of something that you really, really want, something that puts a smile on your face. When you think of your goal, also write down why you want to achieve this goal. The why is a powerful tool that will help you build the connections that will help you keep going when the going gets tough.

Remember, this book is all about feeling better. You are what you attract, thus be great, attract greatness. If you're feeling good, you're going to attract good things into your life. Feeling good NOW is the ultimate objective. Goal setting and thinking about your goals should make you feel AWESOME, as you are thinking about what you want. This should not be a chore; it should be something you are wanting to do and you should feel good. If at any time you are not feeling good, stop what you are doing and start to think of things that make you feel good. A tip for this is to think general. For example, a thought might be, I am growing my belief in abundance, I am becoming better today than I was yesterday, I may not feel great right now, but I am noticing how I am feeling and that is a step to feeling better. Really notice how you are feeling. Most often the feeling of love/abundance/appreciation feels like you have let go of all of your problems, and you feel good energy flowing through your body, connecting your brain with your heart and spreading over your body. You will feel in the moment and powerful, and you will feel some of the best feelings you have ever felt in your life. If you're not feeling great, not to worry, it just means you might not be there yet. The goal could be too big for you to currently believe, or you might not be in the right frame of mind. If this is the case, stop and try again later, or, what has worked for me, is to dive into self-development, as this has always helped me get unstuck and has given me the tools to believe more in myself and my goals.

A quick way to start to feel better is to notice how you are feeling and reach for a feeling that is a little better. You won't be able to go from depressed to the feeling of love and joy just like that. Just search for a better emotion than you currently have been feeling. Example, if you have been feeling depressed or jealous, then searching for the feeling of anger is actually a better feeling than depressed or jealousy. If you are feeling contentment, then passion and or enthusiasm would be a better emotion to strive for. The key is to be aware of how you are feeling when you're thinking your thoughts, because if a thought is making you feel good, think more of it, and if a thought is making you feel bad, let it go. I know it's not always easy to let go of something you probably care a lot about, and that is why you are thinking the thought, but the more you worry and stress about your problem, the more attention you give it, the more it will grow. There is plenty to be grateful for. Can you see the good in your life, is the question?

Why am I talking about searching for feelings when talking about goal setting?

I am talking about the feelings, as it is a MUST that you feel good about your goals. When you think of your goals, you should feel powerful and excited, as the feelings will lead you to get what you want.

Here is a tip: if you are broke, in debt of thousands of dollars, and your goal is to become a millionaire, this is very possible; your BELIEF level has to be without a doubt that you will achieve your goal. When I was going through the process and first writing down large goals, I found myself at times not believing that I could get there. It took myself really having faith in the process and visualizing over and over again what life would be like in achieving this goal. The more I visualized, the more my confidence grew that my dreams were coming to reality. The secret really is, when you think of something you really really want, you should feel free/excited, exhilarated and it's the feeling that you need to harness. If there is anything that I want you to take out of this chapter, it's the feeling that you get when you think of your goal that will bring you the success. To know and have the confidence that you can achieve the feeling of feeling free/excited, exhilarated whenever you want, will increase the belief in your goal. Remember, whatever you feel, life will bring you more of those feelings. So, if your goal is small and you just feel good, that is ok, just know that when you focus on your goal, your going to get good things flowing into your life, but if you feel amazing, amazing things will flow into existence. The reason why I am talking about setting a big goal, and why there is a plethora of research on this, is because by thinking of a big goal, you will have a higher probability to continue to work towards that goal. It's easier to remember to focus on something that gets you excited, rather than something that you don't really care about. Not to mention, the longer you work towards your goal, the more challenges that you will face, the more you will grow to be the person you desire to become. Once you understand the process of dreaming big, then give it a shot; you will see more success when your dream gets you really excited. At the same time, it's as easy for you to attract one dollar as it is one million dollars; it's simply what belief level you have. The sense of knowing about you are what you attract, will give you the confidence to call upon the feelings of your goal more often, which will deliver more focus towards your desire and more excitement to work towards what you want. In fact, the work will not seem like work, it will be a desire to live. Confucius once said, "when you love what you're doing, you will never work a day in your life".

As you are thinking about your goals and feeling how great it is once its achieved, you will become "in alignment" with what you want. When you can get perfectly in alignment with what you want, then this is where your goals will come in at lightning speed. The more you get aligned, the quicker you will reach your goal. How will you know when you're aligned? You will know when you know. It's a feeling of knowing. It's a feeling of pure joy, appreciation, excitement, and confidence. To understand that vibration precedes manifestation is key to this process, and I will talk about this more in the next chapter, Belief.

Ten-year plan

Here is another tip: create your 10-year plan. Where do you see yourself in 10 years? Really think about what you want your life to look and feel like. The more specific the better. Ten years is a long time. Thinking 10 years ahead can allow you to believe it is possible to achieve anything because of how our brain perceives the duration of time. Also, imagine yourself actually working and staying focused on one goal for 10 years—man, that is a long time with intense focus. But imagine you did and could keep your focus on something for that long. This is why the goal needs to be big; you will start to master your craft, and once your goal is achieved, you will know that you did that; you have the power to create. If you set your goal at attracting one hundred dollars in your life, would you really know that you did that or would it be because of some random circumstances. I know many people who start businesses, and four years later they have created retirement money. Here is a fun game: take a look at Amazon and Tesla stock. Google them and see how much their stock grew in 10 years.

The 10-year thinking ahead can allow you to believe that it is possible to achieve anything. The belief is key. Remember, your brain doesn't know the difference between what is real and what is fake. Create the images and create the feelings of what you want your life to be and you will act as a magnet to attract more of these feelings, which will, in turn, create more of what you want in your life.

Next, take your 10-year plan and have a powerful reason why you want to achieve this goal. A powerful *why* can carry you through the muddy waters. My mom has a crazy story. My dad spent his career in the medical devices field as a manager of a spine division at Stryker Canada. He was in charge of a billion-dollar revenue stream . . . stressful. Ultimately, the stress and pressure (mixed in with bad diet and hereditary), led him to have two heart attacks when he was 49 years old. My mom knew that if she didn't make enough money to retire him from the job, she would be without her husband. At that time (the year was 1997), she wrote a cheque for one million dollars and put a date of October 31, 2001 on it, and stuck it on the fridge. She looked at this every day, and remembered why she was doing what she was doing (to keep her husband alive). Back then, my parents were making ends meet, but by no means anywhere close to retirement as they had debt and a mortgage to pay off. My mom decided to be a distributor in a network marketing company. She had no experience, but she had heard of the financial payoffs in network marketing. (Side note, only about 1-3% of people who join a network marketing company actually make the top life-changing money). Four years later to the date (actually off by two days), my mom had accumulatively made one million dollars in network marketing, which helped retire my dad from his line of work and ultimately saved his life. First off, why did my mom succeed when so many people fail in network marketing? A couple of big reasons are, she wrote down her goal, looked at it daily, but even more importantly she knew why she wanted this goal, and the why is what created the feelings to help her achieve success.

I saw my dad when he officially retired, roughly two or three days later, and he looked 10 years younger. It was like pounds of baggage and stress had left his body. He looked fresh—something I hadn't seen my dad look like in decades.

It seemed crazy, though, that my mom had reached her goal of making one million dollars, when there was no possible way that she could have earned that kind of money or that she could think of it and that she was only two days off from the date she had written on the imaginary cheque. That just goes to show that there is some serious magic/power behind goal setting and visualization. This leads to my next point.

Write your goals in the present tense, as you are what you attract. When you write your goals, this is where you have to believe you can achieve them. "Whatever the mind can conceive and you can bring yourself to believe you can achieve." (Napolean Hill 1937). For me, goals are written like this, as examples: I am mortgage free, I am a millionaire, I am attracting the feeling of abundance, I feel grateful for _____. The key, when you are writing in the present tense, is to see if you can get an image or feeling as you are writing; this will amplify the process dramatically.

There is a story in the movie *The Secret* where Jack Canfield (famous for the book, *Chicken Soup for the Soul*) talks about how he imagined himself every morning and every night living life with $100,000. At the time, he was only making $9,000 per year so $100,000 was nowhere in reach, except in his mind. When the year finished, Jack talked about making $96,000. Was he mad that he was $4,000 shy? Hell no. His wife said, "If this thinking will work for $100,000, then will it work for $1 million a year?" Sure enough, it did.

I hope that after reading these stories, and having an understanding of the power of writing down what you want, you have thought of something that you truly desire and why you want such a thing. Before you move on to the next chapter, write down your BIG goal and why you want to achieve what it is you want.

CHAPTER 2

BELIEF

What do I want you to get out of this chapter?

I want you to have trust/faith/belief in a higher power, even if that higher power is yourself. Without this, I am not sure how you will be able to get your mind to a spot of achieving the feeling of knowing your dreams are coming true, especially when I hope you will be setting your goals extremely BIG; goals that would be impossible to achieve right now in your current state of being.

I also want you to understand that you have an unlimited power to be connected to source energy to make your dreams a reality. Some call being connected as living in the present, aka, living in the NOW. You can feel it. It's also the spot where pure love, positivity, creativity, and appreciation live. The NOW is a spot of feeling really good and really alive. The NOW is also known as the VORTEX by some. The vortex is the spot where everything you have ever desired exists. Your dreams, your goals, every good feeling you could imagine are in your vortex. The more you can get connected and live in the present moment, the faster your dreams become reality.

I also want you to understand and believe in the Law of Attraction. It's a Universal Law proven by Quantum Physics. This is a known fact. The Law of Attraction states, like attract likes. In other words, your thoughts become things. Whatever you think about most of the time, becomes your reality. If you think good things will happen, most often good things happen. On the contrary, if you think negatively most of the time, bad things constantly happen in your life. Knowing the Law of Attraction is the first step, and becoming aware of your thoughts is one of the first things you can do. Don't worry— manifestation does not happen right away, and it's been proven that a positive thought has a hundred times more power than a negative thought; so don't worry too much about all those negative thoughts that come into your mind. Actually, it's good to have some negative thoughts, as they can provide you with contrast, and the more you know about what you don't want, the closer you will get to having thoughts about what you do want. So appreciate the bad thoughts, and use them as a trigger to think more about what you actually want. How do you know if a thought is good or bad? It's all about how it makes you feel, and this is the trick that we will talk about later, as often we think we are thinking what we want, but we are really thinking the lack of that thought, which is bringing into our life more of what we don't want.

Getting back to what I want you to take away from this chapter, belief is about having faith in the Universal Laws, and that the universe is here to help you achieve what you want. We call this having faith. Really though, faith is just an understanding of how the universe really works; vibration precedes manifestation. Without going too much into science and Quantum Physics, every thought and everything on earth is connected and has a vibration. There are many studies that prove the Law of Attraction, and it is now a fact that we have the ability to change the way things are, with our thoughts. Google Dr. Masaru Emoto's experiments on how we have a dramatic effect on changing the crystallization of water with only our thoughts. You get a different crystallization depending if the thought is negative compared to positive. This is just one of many studies done by many doctors and (or) Quantum Physicists.

So where do I start?

Your job is to surrender your dreams as if you already know that they are going to happen. When you are in the Vortex the NOW, it allows you to feel the appreciation for what is and the anticipation for what's coming. The ultimate feeling of when you are living in the present moment will make you feel like you have everything, and when you feel like you have everything you will need nothing. Ironically, when you feel like you need nothing, because you feel like you have everything, is when your dreams start rushing into your life.

There is no need to sweat or worry about your dreams not going to happen, as that would be a thought coming from disbelief. If there is an ounce of doubt, trust me when I say, your goals will not become a reality. You must come from a place of knowing. That is why having faith and believing is so important, because it will help bring you to a place of certainty. Really, all a belief is, is a thought ingrained in you so deep that you live with certainty, knowing that what you believe will become reality. Every successful person I know lives in a place of certainty. They know that regardless of their situation, regardless if they are against all odds, they will come out on top. Even if that means there is only a one percent chance of succeeding, the belief in themselves prevails. Imagine you knew, without a doubt, that you would wake up a millionaire tomorrow. If you could 100% bring your mind to a place of knowing 100%, the manifestation would start to take place (there is a delay and it takes time). The problem is most people have a hard time bringing their mind to such a place of belief. Yeah right, I can wake up with a million dollars in my pocket. It's also hard for many to think this way because we spend so much time seeing our current physical world. If you're looking at your bank account and you barely have enough money for your next coffee, your reality starts to set in. Start with something you can believe in that will happen; this will increase your confidence in this power. Maybe your goal is to wake up tomorrow and someone is going to buy you a coffee. Really get into a place where you believe and know this is going to happen and you are tasting the coffee and seeing yourself say thank you as you take your first sip. Here is the thing, it's as easy for the universe to deliver one dollar as it is one million dollars, it's just what do you believe and what do you know? The other thing I want to add is that you have to live your goal. For example, if you want to be a millionaire, you have to believe you are a millionaire. What does a millionaire think about? How does a millionaire act? Do you live in abundance? Do you stress over your phone bill or mortgage? Remember, the Law of Attraction states that like attracts like, so first you have to have the ability to be who you want to be. When you ask yourself who I am, what responses in your brain come flowing in?

Here is one of my stories on increasing my belief

First off, I have only been to church two times in my life—once for a wedding and one time at Christmas. There is nothing wrong with going to church; the only reason I bring this up is when most people think of what they believe in, they think of going to church and praying to GOD, or at least this is what I have thought. I want you to know, there are other ways. When I first got married and moved into our townhouse, my wife (Carrie) and I created a vision board. On that vision board were things like our dream house, our future kids and their names, Beau and Cali, and my wife's career in teaching full time. We put our vision board in our room by our closet, a place that we went by every day. Constantly seeing our future on our vision board made me feel good. Without knowing, as we look back, seven years later, we had moved out of our house and into our dream house with our kids Cali and Beau. I didn't even realize that we had moved into our dream house until my mom took a picture of the vision board, sent it to me, and I saw that it looked identical to the house we were living in. Subconsciously, we had programmed our minds to start working towards what we wanted. Even though I was at a point where I was working on my belief of being able to achieve anything I desired, I had done enough leg work to program my brain. Also, at that stage of my life, I really didn't have any worries to hold me back. I had little responsibilities, a good job, a good relationship, and I had a vision of what I wanted. Life just happened and started giving me what I was looking for. After realizing that I was living in my dream house, having a boy and a girl, both with the names we had thought of seven years prior, and that Carrie was working where she had always wanted to work, it took my belief to the next level. A huge side note here, all of this takes work and energy, but when your belief level is high and you start to go with the flow of things, all the work to achieve these goals seems effortless.

My ability to allow what I wanted to come into existence was great, even though my belief in the Law of Attraction was minimal. Now, with an increased belief in my capabilities, and knowing the secrets, this has allowed me to dream way bigger than I have ever dreamt before.

Roger Bannister

Here is one of my favourite stories about belief. If you haven't heard the name Roger Bannister, you will now. Back in the day, in 1946, Bannister won a scholarship to go to medical school at the University of Oxford. At this time, Bannister was not known as an elite runner; the coaches at Oxford said he had an ungainly walk, and he barely made the third team for middle-distance running. The coaches chose him to be the pacer for the first team, and as he was running, he ended up beating everyone by 20 yards and finishing the mile race in 4 minutes and 30 seconds. This is when he knew that he had a talent. Bannister really dove into running, and, in 1952, he broke the world record at the Helsinki Olympics in the 1500 metres and finished in fourth place. At this time, the record for the mile was 4:01 minutes set in the 1940s. After the Olympics, Bannister decided that he was going to run a sub–4-minute mile. This was unfathomable to people, as, back in the day, doctors and exercise experts said that it was impossible for the human body to run a sub–4-minute mile. In fact, doctors said, "there would be so much blood pumping throughout the body, that your heart would explode". Not only that, John Landry from Australia was the fastest runner at the time; Bannister was an afterthought as he didn't even medal in the Olympics. Bannister did not accept this belief that he would die and that it was impossible to run a sub–4-minute mile. He thought that if someone could run a mile in 4:01 that it was close enough that you could run the mile in 3:59. Bannister knew with his medical background that it was not a physical limitation that was holding people back from breaking the barrier, but rather a psychological barrier. Bannister constantly practiced and he also visualized the achievement he was seeking in order to create a sense of certainty in his mind and body. One year later, Bannister ran the mile in just over 4 minutes. Failing to reach his goal, he said that it gave him more belief that he could run a sub–4 minute mile. With much practice and visualization of achieving his goal, on May 6th, 1954, Bannister ran the mile in 3:59.4 minutes.

This is a story of resetting the bar of possibilities and believing what is possible. The funny thing is, after he completed this, just 46 days later, his record was broken. Now over 4,000 people have run a sub–4 minute mile. Running the mile in under 4 minutes is now the standard for middle-distance runners. Currently, the world record for running the mile is 3 minutes and 46 seconds. I hope this story gets you to challenge your beliefs and release the stories and excuses that are holding you back from achieving your goals, as if you truly believe, anything is possible.

More about belief

Having absolute belief is really a state of knowing. It's trusting that everything happens for a reason and is meant to happen. Even if something bad happens, look at the so-called bad situation and realize that the "bad thing" is only bad in your mind. Maybe a horrible experience will teach you something that you need to know to make your dreams a reality. Maybe it's little, like a traffic jam and you're late for your party. Maybe the traffic jam stopped you from getting into a worse situation like a speeding ticket or an accident. With having the belief and the attitude that right now you are in the perfect place at the perfect time to achieve your goals is a powerful feeling. Think on how confident you will be if you knew that your dreams are coming true right now, as if everything you have ever wanted is coming to you right now. You will feel 10 feet tall and bulletproof. You will exude confidence because you know that life is great, and having the sense of knowing is really believing.

Understand that, even though you know your dreams are coming true, there will be failures, and bad things will happen. It is smart to understand that success is not a straight line up; it looks more like this:

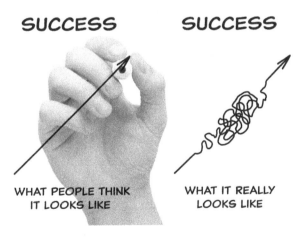

To really understand what success looks like will allow you to appreciate and learn from all the failures that will happen along the road. I know we have most likely seen this picture before, but have we really understood what happens in all those squiggly lines—the feeling of disappointment, the feeling of disbelief, the feeling of failure? These are feelings that you will have to overcome. Understanding that these will happen will hopefully allow you to appreciate the tough times and bring you to knowing that your dreams are closer than you think.

The universe will bring you the experiences you need to face in order for you to achieve your dreams. The universe will also bring you what you need, not always necessarily what you want; but what you need will always be much more powerful than what you think you want.

When will all of this happen? Everything will happen at the perfect time. When you're ready to receive, the lessons will come. "The teacher appears when the student is ready," (Lau Tsu). Your belief in allowing yourself to grow to a place where you can feel the success and feel the knowing is a path that I would strongly encourage. This path will allow you to find your purpose in life, which will allow you to wake up every day feeling excitement.

My purpose—and feel free to use it—is to feel as happy as I possibly can, to feel as much love and abundance as frequently as possible. What better journey is there than to always feel good? The person striving to be a millionaire is really just striving to be a millionaire as he thinks the money will make him feel good/ powerful. The person searching for a soul mate is really searching for a soul mate because they think that person will make them feel loved. It is important to really understand that feeling good is what we are all searching for, and understanding that the better we feel, the better the people around us will feel as well. Being a parent to two amazing kids, I want them to understand what happiness looks and feels like. So for them to see and feel this, it is my duty and responsibility to put effort into allowing myself to grow and be the best possible self I can be. You can only give what you have, thus believe unequivocally and undoubtedly that you are great and the world will give you what you are, greatness.

Here are some tips to get you to be able to live your dream life and achieve your BIG hairy audacious goal:

1. Start small. This will help you to increase your belief in the power of now and the power of the Law of Attraction. Without knowing that you will achieve something, comes doubt. With doubt comes failure. Do what you need to do to find belief in yourself, or in this universe, to help you get what you want. This is why I preach self-development. It seems as though you are on the right path if you are reading this book, as self-development is the key to removing the barriers that are holding you back and helping you believe in all of your greatness. Never stop learning as your powers are limitless.

2. Surround yourself with people that have what you have. This will allow you to more easily visualize what those successful people do in their day-to-day lives. It will

allow you to pick up on their habits that have got them to where they are. Success does not come from one big thing; it's made up of small habits done day in and day out. What new habits are you willing to develop? Maybe it's reading, maybe meditating, maybe working out, maybe spending quality time with loved ones. If you can develop four new small habits a year, by three years you have 12 new habits of success. This is HUGE!

3. Breathe. The more you can release tension and bring yourself to the NOW, the better you will feel, and feeling better is really the secret to attracting what you want in life. The more you can be aware of your breathing, the more you are destressing yourself. Every bad disease, and every worry, is a form of stress. Releasing the stress will make you feel lighter and bring you closer to allowing good thoughts to come into your life.

CHAPTER 3

ROUTINE

What do I want you to get out of this chapter?

The actions you take in life will lead to who you are and what you have; therefore, to create a routine of good habits will forever change your life for the better. Success is not made of one large thing you do; it's made up of small habits done day in and day out. The habits you create today will determine how your life will be tomorrow. Throughout this chapter, I want to share with you some tips, stories, and ideas that I have learned, as well as what some of the most successful people in the world are doing. Success will leave clues; to be aware of them will create more power and enlightenment than you can imagine.

Here is the story of creating my success habits, which I hope will be a story that many of you can relate to, as it's not all sunshine and riches. I share my journey to developing the habits that have worked for me for a couple reasons. First, there are some key lessons that I have learned along the way about change and developing new habits. Second, maybe I have a habit that you will enjoy. Remember, this is your journey, and what I do may not always work for you or you may not enjoy what I do. Hopefully you can take a nugget or two out of this chapter and start to fast track your life to feeling the best you have ever felt.

I made a decision

Here is a quick story about a decision that I made to help me be the person I am today. At one work party I attended, I had a little too much to drink. By little, I mean, I woke up the next day with the worst hangover of my life. Have you ever woken up and said, "I am never drinking again"? Well, I had said this, but then I thought I really like wine, and I want to be able to have a glass or two if I choose. So I made the decision to take one year off drinking; I wanted to see what I could accomplish with more focus during this time. For me, this was a big deal as drinking was part of my social life. Not like I was an alcoholic, but I really enjoyed having a few casuals, and once in a while letting loose at a party.

Here is what happened. After one month of no drinking, I felt more energized and more clarity then I had ever felt before. The feeling did not increase after the one month, but it sustained for the year and to now. The cool part was, with more energy, it was easier waking up before the kids awoke. Before, I would get into a routine in the morning, but then I would get too tired, or if I went out on a Saturday night, I would feel like crap on the Sunday and maybe the Monday. I would lose all momentum, so then I would try and start my routine back up on Tuesday; sometimes I did and sometimes I didn't. Sometimes I took weeks off as I always felt like I had to start fresh again. Now with no drinking, I got into my success habits more consistently and with more excitement. The more consistent I have been, the better I have been feeling, and the more good things have just appeared in my life. It all started with a decision to feel better and to not drink for one year.

Success Habit 1

I have to start off with talking about working out. When I was 12 years old and lifting the Hulk Hogan weights in my base-ment—doing sit-ups, push-ups, bicep curls—I can remember looking in the mirror and feeling strong. The feeling of making myself stronger, was an addicting feeling. I just felt good. I thank my parents for putting my brother and me into sports. And my dad was a great role model, seeing him work out in the basement. Of all my habits, working out has been my most enduring habit, as I have seen the physical results, but I notice when my body feels good, my mind feels good. I have now worked in the health industry for over 13 years, helping people change their lives. When I realized I could pair my passion with business, that is when I got really excited about my future. I think we all know that there are hundreds of benefits on the body and mind about working out, and as much as I want to talk about them, I suggest if you are really interested in these benefits, to Google "benefits of working out" or read *Living the Good Life* by David Patchell-Evans, as there are 125 reasons to exercise. What I do want to talk about is why I started to work out and what helped me to create this habit at such a young age. First off, my dad and Hulk Hogan were great role models. I just wanted to be strong. I pictured myself growing up to be 6 feet tall and 200 pounds of lean muscle throughout my childhood. I am only 5 foot 9 inches and 185 pounds, so I didn't quite meet that goal, but I'm still proud of my physique. Second of all, I remember going to an indoor soccer game and I saw a spectator, who was roughly 18 years old (I was 12 at the time). His friend called out, "Hey, Derek!"—one of the first Dereks I had heard of, other than myself. I saw him from behind, and he had an extremely long neck. I could relate; I felt I had a long neck as a kid. I had a fear that I was going to grow up with a really long neck, and it did not relate to the image of Hulk Hogan, of whom I had envisioned in my mind. The fear of not turning out the way I had envisioned propelled me to work harder. I know, stupid, but it's true. The third thing that helped me keep working out, was I started to see results. I saw results in the mirror—how strong I felt playing sports (I felt tough). Other people would notice, and I had built some relationships with friends, and it gave me the confidence to have a girlfriend for the first time. Once the results came pouring in, I knew I would never be able to stop. Now, 26 years later, I am still going strong. What I want you to take out of this story is that a lot of things actually came into play with this: I had the personal motivation, I had the social influence, I had the vision, I thoroughly enjoyed what I was doing, and I saw the benefits from the work I was putting in.

Success Habit 2

Fast forward another 12 years to 2006. This was the year I had graduated from Brock University with a bachelor's degree in business. You might be thinking, he didn't create any success habits in university? You are right—not to my knowledge, except I did learn how to live on my own, take care of myself, and I learned how to network. It wasn't until after university that I started to read. My mom gave me the book *The Secret* by Rhonda Byrne. My mom said, "If there is any book you read in your life, I want you to read this one." I took those words to heart. I started reading one page a night. One page became two pages, which soon became a chapter a night. The thing was, I was never a reader. I had never had the desire to learn anything. All those business classes involved theories or formulas or math classes. I got through them because I knew I wanted a degree, because I thought that getting a degree would help me make lots of money, but I never really enjoyed what I was learning. After reading *The Secret*, I discovered my love for self-development. I tapped into a power that I never knew that I had. The book gave me a sense of purpose. I was determined to learn how to control my thoughts, as the book was about the Law of Attraction, which talks about the power of our thoughts. Let's fast forward to the present moment, 14 years later. I still read; I have read roughly 50 or 60 books. I aim for four books a year, sometimes a little more. What I love about reading is it gets my mind going. If you have ever felt like you were, or are, in a rut, reading has always made me feel on top of my game. There is something magical that happens when you read, that gives you a feeling of confidence that you're getting better, that you're on the right track. I am not talking about fiction books (although there are benefits to fiction, such as building your imagination); I am talking about reading self-development books—books designed to help you realize how great you are. Now, you might already realize that you're pretty awesome, and I congratulate you for knowing this, but what I have realized is that most people, including myself, don't even know how awesome they are. We are powerful beyond measure, and frequently I get a taste of the feeling of connectedness and how much power we have to effect change in this world, but it all starts with us. The more you can learn about yourself—about who you were before the noise of society, before life hits you with bills, worries, your job, kids, relationship—the more you can bring yourself back to having the light and excitement you once had as a child. The sooner you get to that level of excitement, the sooner you will realize how amazing this life really is and its untapped potential to have anything you want.

Success Habit 3

Meditation has been a big part of my journey. I once heard, "If you don't have control over your mind, your mind has control over you." The goal of meditation is to release all thoughts and to clear your mind to bring yourself to a conscious state. Once you can still your mind, you can be more aware of the present moment, and when you're enjoying the moment, there are no worries, no problems; you have everything you could possibly need. Knowing this, I started to meditate. I would meditate for about 15 minutes a day, for about 3 days a week. This lasted for a couple of months, and then it became here and there where I would meditate. Eventually, I stopped when we had our first child. I stopped making time for myself. Funny thing was, when I stopped making time for myself, all the benefits I was receiving from feeling on top of my game, like feeling successful at work, feeling confident, having no stress, and feeling like life was working for me, came to an end. Having to adjust to a new life with a child was not easy, as all I wanted to be at that moment was a great dad. When I stopped meditating, I noticed a bit of stress coming into my life: financially, we had made a bad investment, work was just all right, and I was feeling exhausted. After a couple of years of feeling sub-par, I knew I had to have my time to develop myself, to make myself better. I started waking up at 5:30 every morning, and that gave me roughly one hour to myself. At first, it was a little hard, as I was fighting the tired bug, but knowing that I could only give what I had constantly came into my brain. I knew that if I wasn't feeling my best, my family would suffer, and I wouldn't be the best dad or best husband I could be. I knew things had to change. I got back into the habit of meditating first thing in the morning, and I have stuck with it ever since. At this point, I have been meditating for over a year straight daily. I find that conquering myself is the best way to start my day. If I can conquer myself to start the day, then the rest of the day will be a breeze. What I learned to keep this habit up was thoroughly enjoying what I was doing and knowing why I wanted to do it. The more I meditated, the more I started to feel better and better, to a point where any free time I had, I wanted to meditate because it felt so liberating. Yes, there were thoughts of becoming a monk, then reality kicked in. No joking aside, the ability to let go of all thoughts, bringing yourself to a pure conscious state, is one of the most powerful things you can do. There are studies out there that when you can truly bring yourself to a conscious state, there are readings of your brain omitting millions of mega bolts of energy. Normally, most people will omit 40 to 60 mega bolts of energy in their day-to-day lives. I will say this again, when you meditate and bring yourself to a conscious state, you can omit millions of mega bolts of energy. Dr. Joe Dispenza talks with the latest research in neuro science that, the energy that you omit is enough energy to cure any disease, heal broken bones, realign the body to live pain free, it's enough energy to create anything you desire. He also says that, "the power that made the body, heals the body". If you don't know who Dr. Joe Dispenza is, please Google him as he has an incredible story of healing himself as he was hit by a semi truck during a triathlon, breaking multiple vertebrae and was told that he would never walk again. With the power of meditation and visualization, he reconstructed his spine one vertebrae at a time.

From a documentary called Heal, Dr's are saying that the best science of our time is now showing that every organ has the ability to heal itself.

Buddah says, " every man and woman is the architect of their own healing." We all have this power, the question is what do you believe? Can you bring your mind to believe in a future that you can't see or experience with your senses? To be more connected with the energy of your future than your energy from what is going on will bring you the vibrations you will need to start to heal yourself. The feeling of wholeness, is where the magic begins. Dr. Joe Dispenza states, "the intelligence that gives us life, is the greatest healer in the world, all we have to do is get our of the way".

Success Habit 4

I am saying this loud and proud, "I AM A JOURNALER!!" I never imagined I would journal my thoughts, until I heard about the power of journaling. When you write things down, the connections between your hand and brain help create and deepen the neural pathways in your brain. Why is this so important? Our subconscious brain controls 99.9% of everything that we do, so our job is to fill our brains with what we want and our subconscious will go to work for us 24 hours a day, 7 days a week. Our brains never stop working; the question is, are our brains working for us or are they working against us? After I meditate, I grab my coffee and I journal. I usually write about three pages of stuff. I write down affirmations, goals, intentions, things I am grateful for, and I ask myself questions—whatever I need to write to bring myself to a point where I feel absolutely amazing. Who is going to pump you up on a daily basis? Most people will go each day without anyone telling them how good they are; over time self-doubt or unworthiness can creep in. Why not journal about things you're proud of or things that make you feel good? I love asking myself a question to a problem that I am having or a question on what I need today to make me feel even better. When you ask yourself a question, your brain has to answer it. I just write whatever comes to my mind and what I have noticed is, I always know the answer to any question that I ask myself. All I have to do is listen to my thoughts and write out what comes flowing in. This is why I like to mediate before I journal to bring my mind to a place of peace where there is no, or limited, noise, as I can easily hear the answers that start flowing into existence. What keeps me journaling, is the feeling I get when I have built myself up to a point where I know that I am going to make a positive impact on people's lives, as just being around me will brighten their day.

Here are some tips to creating a routine that you will stick with

I have failed many times at sticking with my good habits, because change is hard; but the most important thing is to find enjoyment in your process. I love my routine so much that I would not miss it for anything . Whether you're drinking a coffee while journaling or doing whatever you do—or understanding why you are doing what you are doing—whatever it is, if you don't love it, as soon as it gets tough or you get tired, you will fail. By learning to push through the resistance points when you feel like you're bored or when you feel like giving up, you will learn self-discipline and resilience. I look at Tiger Woods as a great example of this characteristic. There are videos of Tiger on the driving range in the pouring rain, during tournaments and even on his own time. Do you think other professionals at that time were on the range with him? Tiger rose to the top and he had the discipline to do the things no one else was willing to do.

When I was younger, I used to golf 120 rounds a year at the Brantford Golf and Country Club. We would have a blast. We also golfed with many good golfers. There were three or four golfers who had some serious potential to make golf their profession. One of the golfers was David Hearn. David, in my eyes, was not the best of the top golfers. But he was always practicing when the other golfers played more. I would see David there at 6:30 a.m., when I would arrive, and when I would leave at 7:00 p.m., he was still there practicing. David was the only one to make it to the PGA out of the group of elite golfers at our club. David had the discipline to hit more balls at practice and fine tune his craft than others. He was laser-focused on what he wanted, and he didn't let anything stop him from accomplishing his goals.

How will I know if I love it or not?

The biggest thing I found is that the more I read, the more I journaled, the more I worked out, the more I meditated, the easier it got and the better I felt. At the start, you most definitely will find a new habit tough, as it's different from what you have been doing before, but the more you do it, the easier it gets. If you can get to the point where you don't want to miss a day or feel guilty for not doing it, that is when you love it. What has worked for me is consistency. Whatever new habit you are choosing to embark on to better your life, five days a week has always seemed to work for me. I feel that whenever I have failed, it's because I would choose to do something three days a week, and three became two, which became zero pretty fast. Five days a week seems to be the magic number.

Start small. When I first started reading, it was more important that I developed the habit of reading, and I only read one page a day. The habit of picking up the book was the hard part. When I started meditating, 15 minutes a day was all I would aim for. Now, I meditate for as long as possible, but 15 minutes per day, minimum. When you first start working out at the gym, going is the hardest part. Once you're there, go easy, just gain confidence slowly, and only think about developing the habit of going to the gym.

Lastly, educate yourself on the how-to's and the benefits of doing what you're doing. Educate yourself on the reasons why you want to develop the habits. If you know why and you know the benefits of doing what you're doing, you're much more likely to stick with the habit. If you fail at your habit, it's okay, it's not the end. You will be ready when you're ready. Everyone's on their own journey, at their own pace. It wasn't until I was 36 that I got into the best habits of my life. It's never too late to start to feel amazing; the time is NOW.

Here is the cool part.

What I have learned about myself through developing these habits was a surprise. By understanding myself better, and being on the journey to bettering myself, I have found my purpose, which I spoke about in the previous chapter. It is my goal to feel as good as possible so that my kids can understand what happiness looks and feels like. So waking up at 5:30 a.m. might seem daunting to some, maybe not, but if you had asked me a couple years ago, 5:30 did not exist in my world, and now it is easy for me as I wake up with passion and excitement every day. I feel like I have a duty to get better, and consequently that duty to get better makes me feel damn good and I know that others around me benefit as well.

What does it actually take to build a habit?

Believe it or not, there is a science to change. There is a great book out there called *Change Anything* by Kerry Patterson,

Joseph Grenny, David Maxfield, Ron McMillan, and Al Switzler, which talks about the new science of personal success.

The book talks about six sources of influence, including personal ability and motivation, social ability and motivation, and structural ability and motivation. The biggest thing I took from the book was in order for change to last, you need to have four of the six boxes.

Picture a tug of war with three people on each side, with each side representing one of the above boxes. If there were three people with equal strength on each side, the tug of war would last until you got tired. You would eventually lose the battle because you cannot go on forever feeling exhausted. Now, picture four people on one side and two people on the other; you're going to win the majority of the time. So in order to make a change, you need to have more things helping you out than going against you. But the reason why most people fail at making a change—say it's exercising or trying to quit smoking—is because four things can actually be a lot. Four things might be having the personal motivation to make a change, having support from your family and friends, setting up a reward system for yourself, and having the know-how to accomplish the task. The reality is most people don't know what it takes to make a change so they don't do enough to make the process easy for themselves. If you want more clarity on the six-source model, *Change Anything* is a phenomenal read.

So where do I start?

First off, make a decision for the change you are looking for. With making a decision and having a vision of what you want life to look and feel like, you are programming your mind to give it direction to start travelling towards that vision.

Next, pick a couple—up to four—habits to create for yourself. What worked for me is exercising, reading, meditation, and journaling. I would say, even just pick one or two new habits; we are all on our own journey; there is no race; it's what feels best for you. With that in mind, if you do have a sense of urgency to accomplish your goals, there is a lot of power in that as well, but do what is best for you.

Then, whatever you do, remember a couple of important things about your chosen new habits:

1. Have a reason as to why you are doing them—write down the reason (there will be some days when you feel like you're getting stuck in the mud), and, if you're WHY is not big enough, you will forever be stuck. You need a reason.

2. Do them every day. For example, if reading is your new habit, read at least one page each day. If meditation is your new habit, meditate for at least five minutes every day. If it's working out, and say you can only get to the gym two or three times per week, maybe you do five minutes of push-ups or stretching at your home or office or in front of the TV while watching your favourite show or during the commercials. Daily habits are the key to success, so incorporate them into

your day. There is nothing more important than feeling good now. MAKE YOURSELF A PRIORITY.

What if I don't know how to effectively do one of my new habits?

Hire a personal trainer, use Google, ask someone who you know who successfully does a habit that you are looking to get into. Having the ability to perform the habit is one of the boxes in the formula for *Change Anything*. With that being said, there is no bad action. Action will give you clues. There is no bad workout, there is no bad meditation, there is no bad journaling session, there is no bad day of reading. You will and should feel good regardless of whether you did not maximize your session. Although, can you imagine maximizing each new habit and how good you will feel once you get the change you're looking for? I highly encourage investing in yourself as your investment will pay off ten-fold. Imagine throwing a stone in the water, and the first ripple is the investment, but as time happens you see the ripple effect and the waves getting bigger. The same thing happens as you grow; you start to have more effect on your world and the people around you.

Final thoughts

To know that your thoughts control your feelings, that your feelings control your behaviours, and that your behaviours give you the results in your life is a powerful thought. Start with the decision on what you desire, and work from there. With knowing why you want what you want, your new habits will come with great ease. Yes, there will be resistance at the start, as it's something new, and developing the neural pathways in your brain takes time, but once you are there, I hope you thoroughly enjoy your habits, as it's a lifelong process. Remember Tiger Woods: he loves golf, and the habits that he performs day in and day out have helped him be questionably the greatest athlete of all time. This goes hand-in-hand with the saying, do more of what you love and you will never work a day in your life. My suggestion to you is that when you're making a decision to find the desire you are looking for, make the decision to be the best self you can be, as the habits you create to live your best life will foremostly be a decision that will feel good. When you feel great, you attract greatness.

CHAPTER 4

POSITIVITY

What do I want you to get out of this chapter?

Ultimately, I want you feeling better. After reading this chapter, I hope to give you another perspective to start adding more positivity into your life. I want you to realize that you have a lot more control and power than you think, and it all starts with that small voice in your head and the thousands of choices you make every day. You have the ability to control your thoughts, and your thoughts ultimately control what your life looks like; therefore, isn't it better to be thinking of things that make you feel good, rather than thinking about the problems in your life? In this chapter, I want you to realize that you once had the power of optimism, but, over time, with life stressors, you have somehow slowly started to lose the power of positivity. Your job now is to get back what you once had and to watch your life change for the better.

*Okay, this seems like hard work and I am on a long streak
of bad things happening. How am I supposed to change?*

Here is the thing, anyone can be more positive and optimistic as we all have control over our thoughts, it just might take building new habits of thinking to release the old bad thoughts. Here is a little test that I encourage you to do before you continue on with this chapter. Take out a blank piece of paper, and take three minutes to write down all the things that are great in your life, or all the things you love. This can be gratitude for your home, your friends, your family, your job, your paycheque, the air we breathe, the clothes on your back; really, write down anything that makes you feel good, and circle them. Go . . .

Your page should be filled with circles. Now draw a small black dot on the top right corner of your page. This small black dot will represent a problem that you face in life or something that bothers you. Now look at the page. What does your attention go to? How are you feeling?

What I have noticed in doing this exercise over the years and from having friends and colleagues do the exercise, is that oftentimes our attention goes to that small black dot and we start to worry and feel bad. When really that small black dot is just a tiny space compared to focusing on all the great things in our life that we love. If we can focus more on the things we love and feel good, watch the problem go away. "How will the problem go away?" you may ask. When you focus on the things that make you feel good, you start to attract more of what feels good into your life. Here is an example. Say the small dot is a financial dot, and you need more money to pay bills. When you focus on things you love, things such as job opportunities, random cheques or savings start to come into existence. I know this sounds weird and you might not believe this, but when you let go of the problem, the universe starts to go to work for you to give you the tools to learn how to solve the problem.

Let me give you an example of how toddlers think to show you that we have developed the ability to worry and stress over our problems.

This is just an example on how we have developed negative neural pathways, which serve us no good. My son had a fever of 102 to 103. Temperature-wise, he was really sick. My wife and I were giving him Tylenol to lower the fever. It would work for a short while and then it would come back to the same high temperature. We decided to take him to the doctor, just to be safe. They swabbed his mouth to test to see if he had strep throat. Sure enough, two days later, it was confirmed he had strep throat. Here is the cool part, over all this time (four days of having the fever) we would always ask him, how he was feeling and his response every time was "I feel happy." By the way, he is two (almost three). Regardless, he doesn't know much more than to feel happy.

Children shine all the time. They are pure joy and love. If you don't have kids or you're not around kids, picture a dog's love and joy. When I get home from work, my kids are at the door screaming, "Daddy"; they jump on me and give me a hug and a kiss, basically the same thing as a dog. What I am getting at is that we all had this positivity and we all have developed beliefs of limitations which has made many of us unhappy at some point. It's in us; we just have to remember, deep down, who we really are to remember the joy in life.

This still seems like it's going to be really hard if I have been looking at the glass half empty for so long, to now all of a sudden change my thoughts?

On the contrary. First off, you don't need to be thinking positive thoughts 100% of the time, not even 80%, not even 60%. All you need to do is to think positively 51% of the time. If you can create 51% positive thoughts, then you are thinking more positive thoughts than negative. Once this happens then momentum can start, then 52%, 55%, 58%—now you are starting to notice more good things coming into your life, which makes you think and feel more appreciation, which again fills your day with more positivity.

What if I am so far on the negative scale, thinking 80% negative and 20% positive—what then?

First off, a good way to recognize where your thinking is at is to look around. Do this right now. Look at your life, look at your house, look at the room you're living in, your financial situation, your job, your friends—really look at your life. Are you happy with what you see? Are there areas for improvement? If there are areas of improvement then this next little bit will be for you, as there are direct correlations between if you are thinking positively in an area and you being happy compared to if you feel bad and think negatively in an area and you are struggling. Let's say your bank account is not where you want it to be; I am going to guess that you feel bad when you spend money. I am also guessing that you get stressed out and you are worrying about your financial situation, rather than being thankful for what you have and feeling abundant and appreciative at times.

If you really are not happy with multiple areas of your life and bad things seem to happen to you all the time, here are some good tips to make some change right away.

Meditate for 15 minutes each day. This immediately starts to release any pressure or tension that you might be holding onto, which will in turn raise your positive vibrations. Over time, meditation can really quiet your mind and bring you to a place of self-actualization. Once you start to realize who you are (the childlike joy and appreciation) you will begin to realize how much control and power you have. You will realize that you have abundance inside you, you will realize how connected you are with the universe, you will realize there is unlimited love and happiness. This is so important nowadays as there is so much noise going on in our brains. We watch TV, we listen to music, we listen to our co-workers, family, friends; there is so much noise constantly going on that we need to quiet our minds to regain control. Remember, if you don't have control over your mind, your mind has control over you.

When I first started to meditate, I had no idea how, so I Googled how to mediate, and I found what worked for me. I personally wake up at 5:30 every day, I go downstairs in peace and quiet, and put on a 15-minute YouTube guided meditation. This works for me. Find what works for you. Whatever you choose, it's POWERFUL.

Another thing you can do, right now, is take one of your biggest problems in your life right now. Think about it, really bring it to light, and, here is the kicker, APPRECIATE it. As hard as this is, really find a way to appreciate your problem. Problems do not exist when we give them appreciation. When you face your fears and send them love and appreciation, the fear starts to dissolve. I know this may sound crazy, but who knows, maybe that problem you have been dwelling on has led you to this point right now, where you are about to start to learn the power to dissolve problems and start attracting solutions. You have a long life to live, and there is no better time than right now to begin understanding how to crush your problems and start attracting solutions that can dramatically change your life. So, if you think about it, you're either thinking about something that you want, which makes you feel good, or you're thinking about something you don't want, which makes you feel bad, but, having the ability to recognize your bad thoughts and give them appreciation, you will start to feel good again. Remember, the secret to having anything you want in life is to feel good. Catching yourself thinking bad thoughts takes time, especially if you have been in the habit of thinking about things that worry you. Don't worry about how long it takes, as it's a process that's different for everyone. Hey, if you only catch yourself once today thinking about something that makes you worry or feel bad and you give it appreciation, you are winning. The key is to now be aware of your thoughts, and this is again why mediation helps, as it will make you more aware of how you are feeling. Also, I am sure you have heard that you grow in the face of a challenge. I challenge you to send your biggest fear/problem love and appreciation. Watch it start to dissolve. This problem you have could lead to your greatest gift.

If this is too scary or too hard to contemplate at the moment, start to write down things that you appreciate. Make a list. I am sure you can think of one thing to be grateful for. Maybe it's even I am alive and breathing, maybe it's I am reading and learning right now, maybe it's I have the sight to see these words—who knows. Maybe it's an affirmation of I am not there YET, but I am growing, I am hopeful, I am better today than I was yesterday.

Ultimately, you would want to write out a gratitude list every day, or say and feel this in your mind either last thing before bed or first thing in the morning—even better, do both. I think we all know that gratitude is a secret to success, but knowing is not enough; you must be grateful and practice gratitude to start developing an attitude of gratitude. Develop an attitude for gratitude and watch your world start to change.

Remember, it's the small habits that create the large success.

How does the Law of Attraction relate to optimism?

Here is a quick answer. If you think bad things, the Law of Attraction states that like attracts like, so you are going to attract bad things into your life. Change your thoughts and things will start to change.

Oftentimes, when we are faced with a problem or a challenge, we think negatively about the problem. This immediately gets us frustrated and puts us in a bad mood. We have all done it, myself included. At work, I used to think, how are we going to hit our sales targets when our show ratio is 30% and our close ratio is 40%? This is going to take an impossible amount of leads to get to our goal, I would tell myself. It wasn't until I started focusing on developing myself and bringing myself to a better feeling that things started to change. I started to feel more grateful for what I did have. I felt better coming into work, my staff could feel my presence, our clients and potential clients noticed how positive our atmosphere was, and things started to change. When we feel good, and when we can change our thoughts and beliefs, the world around us starts to change.

Often what gets us feeling bad about the problem is not being able to find the solution. We spend lots of energy on finding how to solve the problem. We immerse ourselves into finding the answer. If I could make any suggestion with this, start to think of the outcome that you're looking for. It could be the outcome of lots of clients coming into the gym, your bank account full, your relationships prospering. When you do this, not only will you start to feel better, but this is when the magic goes to work. This is when ideas of solving the problem will come into existence. The ideas might not come in that instance, but they will come to you sooner rather than later. Have you ever asked yourself a question and got the answer when you were sleeping in the middle of the night or the next morning? Of course you have. It's happened to all of us. This is what I am talking about. Once you start focusing on what you want, answers start to flow into your existence, as there will be less resistance, and, quite frankly, it just feels better.

Final thoughts

Make it a habit to check your thoughts. Remember, you're only going for 51% positive; the rest will come, trust me, as momentum will be on your side.

You're in the right place at the right time to start receiving everything that you have ever wanted. Once you can bring awareness to your thoughts, they will only be positive thoughts, as you're either feeling good or you're learning from your thoughts, and this mindset will lead you to whatever answers you are looking for in life. Take your problems and look at them as challenges and get excited because when you overcome these challenges, you become ten feet tall and bulletproof.

Be positive; attract positivity.

CHAPTER 5

THE POWER OF IMAGINATION

What do I want you to get out of this chapter?

I want you to understand the power of visualization and the effects that it can have on your life. If your brain is your GPS system towards success, by visualizing what you want, with repetition, it will give your mind a destination to start working towards that goal. By the end of this chapter, I want you to practice visualizing the things you want in life. The more you do so with belief, the happier you will be. Ultimately, I want you to picture yourself living the life you want to live. What does it look like? What does it feel like? How are you talking? How are you showing up? By visualizing what you want and believing that it is possible to live any life you wish, you will start to be on a fast track to living your dream.

Here is the thing, your brain does not understand the difference between what's real and what's fake. It understands images and how you feel based on those images. Your subconscious mind is your control mechanism, and 99.9% of all your actions are controlled by your subconscious mind. If you give your subconscious mind a target of living an abundant life (for example, you know what it looks like and feels like), your subconscious will make this work for you. One thing to understand when practising visualization is the Law of Emergence. The Law of Emergence states that everything is experienced internally, meaning, we already have everything that we want, we just have to unleash the power and surrender to our inner being, totally let go of our ego. Derek Rydall explains this greatly in his book *Emergence*. He talks about how an acorn already has an oak tree inside of it; the oak just has to be activated. The oak does not have to be attracted or created; it has everything it needs to become an oak. We are like the acorn: we have everything we need inside us, we just have to learn to activate the greatness and abundance that already exists. Knowing this, hopefully, will allow you to visualize with more belief that anything is possible, as you have all the abundance and love inside you to get you through any situation and to help you gain confidence in your dreams.

Einstein said it first, "Imagination is more powerful than knowledge." It doesn't matter how much you know, it's the images held in your brain that will give you directions to what actions you need to take. After immersing myself in self-development for all those years, yes, I knew some of these secrets to success, but I didn't really know the secrets until I practiced them and saw the results for myself. Actually, better put, I was remembering these secrets, as we all used to be fully connected to this power and potential, we just seem to lose it over the years as we are unaware of how we are creating our lives.

I have always pictured myself a family man with a beautiful wife, gorgeous house and a job that I love. My advice to anyone practicing visualizing their dream life, is to learn patience. Things and people will come when you are ready to receive. Life does not always bring you what you want, but rather, what you need and it will be better than you could imagine.

Here is the thing, you have to consciously start to use your imagination and practice visualization; if you are not used to using your brain in such a manner, the imagination part of your brain starts to shut down. The saying I have always heard is, "If you don't use it, you lose it." I have found this to be true.

How I started to build up my power of imagination

I took an Udemy speed reading course in 2018. It was phenomenal! The course helped me double my reading speed, and I increased my retention by over 30%. The course was structured whereby 80% of the time spent was training your imagination and memory, while the other 20% was spent learning how to speed read. I thought this was weird, at first, until the course gave me an analogy. Picture your brain like a bucket, and a hose is going into the bucket, pouring words, like water flowing, into your brain; speed reading would be like a fire hose, instead of a regular garden house pouring into the bucket. Our main goal was to first increase the size of the bucket to hold the water from the fire hose so that it wouldn't spill over. Speed reading was actually the easy part; it's building your memory and creating visual images for the words (using your imagination) that was the tricky part.

So, in order to build my imagination, the course gave activities, such as choosing any objection/item (let's say, I chose a pen), taking two minutes and writing down as many uses for the pen as I could. I think I came up with five uses the first time. I continued on and learned that kids can do on average 20 different uses for an object. This is because all they do is use their imagination. A child's imagination is so powerful as they non-stop use their brains to create a life of possibilities. Anything is possible for them, even turning stuffed animals into their best friends. I catch my kids all the time playing either barbies or trucks, talking to themselves, playing out different situations. So cute, but so fun listening to them as their worlds are limitless.

This activity started my process, as I felt my imagination was shut off for a while. After one week, I was able to reach 20 uses per item. It didn't take long to get it back. Using your imagination is a lot like working out. We exercise our bodies to make them stronger, and if we don't lift the weights, we will get weaker. The same thing goes with our imagination: the more we use it, the stronger, easier, and more fun the process will be.

More about why I should build up my skill on using my imagination

Let's start here. Do you think that the ability to create the life of your dreams would make you feel good? Do you think if you felt good, more good things would happen to you? It's contagious; momentum builds! Do you think by feeling good and thinking about what you want would put you in a good mind space to be a better student, parent, and perform better at your job? There are so many positives that come with focusing on what you want.

Here is a great example of the power of visualization. There was a study conducted by Dr. Biasiotto at the University of Chicago, where he took three groups of basketball players. All groups had practiced shooting free throws to get their baseline scores. He broke the groups up with different tasks. Group one would practice free throws every day for an hour. Group two just visualized themselves making free throws. And group three did nothing. After 30 days, the groups took free throws: the first group improved by 24%, the second group, which just visualized, improved by 23%, and the last group did not improve at all, which was expected.

Another good example is Tiger Woods. Tiger has 82 wins on the PGA tour, with 15 being majors. Tiger visualizes every shot before he hits the ball. He stops behind the ball, closes his eyes, and sees himself hitting the ball and landing it perfectly on the green. He does this for every shot; when he does, his brain activates the muscles he needs to fire at the exact moments to make this happen. Tiger is one of the most recognized golfers in the world.

I have the pleasure of working with a former professional football player, and he says the team uses visualization in practices to get them prepared for every possible situation that could occur. I feel if you talk with any top athlete, they all practice visualization to some degree to fully prepare them for excellence.

Another example is the story of Colonel George Hall, who was locked in jail, as a prisoner of war, for seven years. While most would lose their minds over this time, Hall decided to go to his happy place, by visualizing the golf course. Every day and every night, he visualized himself hitting each shot perfectly on his favourite course. Every day he pictured every drive going down the middle of the fairway and every approach shot landing on the green; he visualized himself raking the odd bunker, feeling the wind against his back, and, of course, he visualized the ball going into the hole. When Hall got out of jail, one of the first things he wanted to do was to go golfing. In 1973, he was invited to play at the Greater New Orleans Invitational, where he astoundingly shot a 76. For anyone to know anything about golf, this is really hard to do, even if you golf frequently, and Hall had not golfed in seven years. By mentally playing golf every day during his imprisonment, and despite being 100 pounds lighter after he came out of jail, the visualizations had developed muscle memory based on his imagination.

Another jail story I had heard was about a non-muscular guy in jail who worked out every day curling imaginary weights, squatting with an imaginary heavy weight on his back and doing push-ups while imagining he weighed 400 pounds. After his sentence, he came out a jacked beast. As I am writing this, we are in quarantine as the coronavirus is spreading worldwide. With no weights at the house, I tried this workout and I have to say for someone who works out every day, this was one of the toughest workouts I have had in a while. I can now see how, if our brain thinks there is a heavy weight, we activate all the muscles needed to support ourselves in safely doing a weight-lifting exercise.

These are just examples of what can happen if we use our imagination. Start trying this out. It can and should be fun. It will take work, especially if you're not used to using the imagination part of your brain, but it will get easier. Decide on what you want your life to look like, feel like, and how you would show up to your life if you knew you already had it. They say a picture is worth a 1,000 words, so start creating the pictures to help create the connections in your brain to guide your GPS system. You can think of visualization as the mental blueprint that helps to program your brain.

What are some helpful tips to excel at visualization?

1. First, create a vision board of what you really want. This personally helped me to find the house of my dreams. My mom used a vision board to create wealth.

Remember, she put a cheque for one million dollars on our fridge, with the date of October 31, 2009? She saw that cheque every day, and four years later, she had cumulatively created one million dollars in the company she was with, and she did so within two days of the date on the cheque. Recently, I created a new vision board. There is a mansion. I can see myself walking inside this mansion; I see the kids playing in the basement; I see myself going out on the patio for a glass of wine and thinking how lucky and appreciative I am of this world. Life is good. I also see taking the kids to Disney and I see their excitement. The longer you can imagine what exactly you want, the better, try five to ten minutes per day.

2. Right before bed and first thing you do when you wake up, visualize what you want your life to look like. The more you do it, the clearer the images get, and it also starts your day off right by thinking good thoughts. Where attention goes, energy flows.

3. Do it because you want to do it. This should not be a chore. It should feel really good thinking about what you want. If you aren't enjoying the process, you're not fully believing that you can achieve what you really want. If this occurs, here is my advice: stop doing it and start smaller. Start with something you can believe in. As your confidence grows, go BIG!

4. Second, believe that thoughts become things. Einstein was right (surrender to that thought): "Imagination is more powerful than knowledge." Start to believe in yourself and the Power of Emergence. You have everything that you have ever wanted; to surrender yourself to this knowing, and to let the universe do the work, is one of the most powerful things you can do. Activating the power from within is the key to feeling the energy that transforms the manifestations. When you feel it, and believe it, it will come!

5. Use the power of visualization every day. The more you use it, the more it grows. Use visualization for a meeting you're about to run, or a greeting that you're about to have, or how you want a party to go; use it when you're walking into the house with your family; visualize the love that your family gives you, and feel the love.

6. Focus on yourself first. Visualize yourself being great to attract greatness.

CHAPTER 6

LET LOOSE AND ENJOY
THE MOMENT

What do I want you to get out of this chapter?

Enjoy life like it's your last day. Here is why: when you're having fun, you start to attract more of the things you want in life. Now, I don't mean to go out and party and get hammered all day, every day. What I do mean is the first priority is to feel good now. Plan to have fun in everything you do; failure to plan is planning to fail. What I would love for you to do is find ways to add the element of fun in each thing you do. I want you to enjoy the process. Have you ever noticed anyone who is having fun most of the time, that their life seems pretty awesome? Have you ever noticed anyone who hates their job and just seems miserable all the time, that bad stuff always shows up in their life? Life is short; there is no point in doing the things that you hate, day in and day out, as this is not the recipe to a happy and successful life. The more you are feeling enjoyment, the more you will ultimately allow yourself to attract things that make you feel more exhilarated. If you think life is boring, then stop making it boring. Control what you can control. You have control over your thoughts; your thoughts control your emotions. Your job is to bring attention to all the things you want and allow the feelings to abundantly flow into existence. If you come from a place of having you will receive, if you come from a place of trying to attract (which a lot of people have done, including myself), you come from a place of lack and you start to amplify what you don't have. So let loose, give your body a shake. Turn up the music, feel the rhythm take over your body. Your soul needs this! You need this, treat yourself to some fun as you deserve it!

How do I add fun into my life when my day is filled with work and responsibilities?

This is a good question, but only you can provide the answer. Ask yourself, what do I like to do for fun? For some of you, this might be hard to think about, because it's been too long since you have let loose. For quite some time, I was so focused on attracting all the things I wanted in my life, like money and success in my job, that this was my primary thought. All I could think about was receiving these things; I did not think about having fun, as that would have taken me away from my focus. The reality is, I wasn't feeling good when I was thinking about attracting money and success as I was not aligned. I was coming from a place of feeling powerless; I felt like I didn't have the money and I didn't have the success, as this is what I was missing most in my life. The moment I realized that I am the source of money and I am the source of my own success, my world started to change. Allowing myself to realize I had this power made it easy for me to let loose. I felt powerful; I felt in control. I found myself connecting more. I found myself blaring music and dancing all silly for my wife and kids. I found myself laughing more and living in the moment. Funny thing was that the more fun I was having, the more my life started to improve.

The simple act of realizing you have power, love, and abundance within you, makes the things you may not enjoy doing more fun. This might sound strange, but I want you to picture yourself the most confident and happy you have ever felt. Now, once you can get the image of yourself exuding that good feeling, picture yourself doing the dishes or doing the laundry. Do you see yourself doing or thinking anything different? Hopefully you're picturing yourself in the moment, and when you're in the present moment, you're enjoying the sounds, you're enjoying the silence, you're feeling appreciative for what you have. When you can bring yourself to this state of mind, you will be able to let go of all the things you hate about the chore and thoroughly enjoy the moment. For me, enjoying the moment when I am doing chores entails blaring some old school R&B as loud as possible and shutting off my brain and feeling the good vibes as the music takes over my body.

Let's take business calls, for example. Let's say you hate doing sales or service calls. How can you reverse this feeling and enjoy the process? Well anyone in sales should know that there is a five-step process to sell anything (Google, the five building blocks to success). The first step is called Peak Attitude. Do what you need to do to bring yourself to a place of feeling great, feeling confident. Maybe it's remembering that people want your product or service; maybe it comes down to you just love connecting with people, or maybe it's realizing that you have a gift that you want to share with people. Whatever it is, the first step is to make yourself feel good. Before we can sell to anyone, we must first sell ourselves on what makes us happy. What has worked for me is to make sure my environment suits what I need to do to have a good time. A preferable environment for me is with music, a glass of wine, sitting in the hot tub, underneath the stars on a cool summer night. Can you imagine yourself feeling relaxed, feeling the flow, feeling confident, and making business calls? Do you think the person on the other line will be able to hear your confidence and your enjoyment? How much better will your results be? How many more referrals will you be able to generate? How much happier will your boss be? The key is to find your peak attitude first, by allowing yourself to tap into your confidence, to enjoy the process, and to have fun.

What if you're in a situation where you can't play music, sing, dance, or hop into a hot tub? Very good question. Well my first thought would be to quit your job. If it's not an optimal environment for you to be at your best, then find a way to communicate to your boss the environment that best suits you. My second thought, as it's a more logical thought, is to set a challenging goal for yourself that will help you get better. What worked for me was falling in love with self-development. Fall in love with getting better and by getting better and self-development, I really mean letting go of self-limiting beliefs and having more of an understanding of who I really am. Fall in love with reading, listening to audio tapes; fall in love with meditation, working out, affirmations and hang around with successful people. Here is the reason why: when you're on a journey of self-development, you will start to learn to control your thoughts which trigger your emotions and you will start to realize that you have all the power you need to succeed and have fun. Why does this matter? Remember, thoughts become things. Then, in your environment, whatever it is, you will have the ability to really understand that you can imagine your future. Again, why does this matter? All I am asking is, what if I don't have a hot tub or the ability to let loose when I am at work? Picture you work in a call centre, taking 100 calls a day (I have done this before). This wasn't fun, as it became very monotonous, very quickly. You can't play music, you can't sing and dance, you have no hot tub to jump into. Probably you're in a cubicle, hating your life. (Remember though, every bad thought or situation brings contrast. The more you know what you don't want, brings you a clearer picture on what you do want.) How can self-development help in this situation? Here is what self-development will give you: the ability to find the feeling of appreciation and (or) what you want life to look like, imagining doing the things that you want to do. You can create your future whenever you decide to create it. Your actions first start in your mind. The more you think about what you want, the more quickly it will come to you, and the more fun you'll have doing what your doing. Often it's not our job that is making you unhappy, it's how you feel about yourself. If we can bring ourselves to feel ten-feet tall and bulletproof, then we can get to a point where we are having fun and enjoying each situation we put ourselves in. I have also found that the more self-development I do, the more appreciative I get, and the more I start to live in the moment and find the flow of pure enjoyment.

Why isn't everyone enjoying life to the fullest?
In fact, why do I see people looking so miserable on
my drive to work as I look into their car window?

My view on this is that most people are chasing something they do not currently have, whether that's money, a relationship, the feeling of success. Whatever it is, if your chasing something you don't believe you have, your coming from a place of lack, which is a vicious cycle creating more lack in their life.

Why do I think this? Because I have felt this, and I know what work it takes to bring yourself to an understanding and belief that you already have everything. It takes removing old habitual thoughts to create new ones. It takes surrendering yourself to the feeling of already having everything. For most people, they will never get there; they will always be searching for something that keeps getting further and further away. For others, they might feel contentment, and choose not to want more in life; they are satisfied with what they currently have. I have also felt this, and there will be a time in your life where the feeling of satisfaction and contentment will feel like boredom. This is why I preach about always striving to feel better, because—once we go on this journey—answers, ideas, situations, people, and events start to flow into your life to bring you to enlightenment, making you realize that you have everything you need. Again, I talk about this, because as you feel the power you have, it is so easy for you to have fun, and when you're having fun, you're in the moment, feeling the love and appreciation, and, guess what, you will attract more of that into your life.

The other reason I think most people are not figuring out how to allow themselves to live life to its fullest is that life's stressors are weighing us down. Maybe it's the stress of keeping up with the Jones'; maybe it's financially related stressors, such as bills and not having enough money at the end of the month. Maybe it's health stressors or family stressors; maybe it's just the stress of hating your job. Society seems to add stress, and the older you get without managing stress, it can weigh you down. Now, maybe you have been stressed and not used to having fun for a long time. You are then creating the habits of what you don't like, which, I am sad to say, are taking you further away from what you want. The good news is that all this can change, and it can change quickly. To become aware of how you are feeling can be one of your greatest gifts. Finding a way to be appreciative in your big stressor will be the quickest way to start to feel good. This may sound weird, but often times there is so much to learn from what's weighing you down. Once you learn what you need to learn, maybe just learning that by feeling appreciation gives you the power to instantly feel good.

That key is to feel good now. Remember, you can only give what you have, so fill yourself up as much as possible and do what you need to do to feel as good as possible. The more you focus on yourself, the easier it will be to let go of the stressors and allow yourself to start feeling the power you have from within.

What do I do if I am so far gone I have forgotten how to have fun?

Again, only you can answer how you can have fun and enjoy the process, but here is what I did. I can say life gets busy when you have children. I remember when my kids were three and one. I was in such a routine of going to work, and working when I got home, I was either busy with the kids or cleaning something or just too exhausted to do anything. I forgot to focus on myself for a little while. It wasn't until our shifts changed at work, when we had to work one Saturday a month, that I noticed. I am used to having weekends off with the family, but these new hours forced me to take a Friday off. On Fridays, the kids were at school and my wife was always working; I now had some me time for the first time in forever! It was quiet, peaceful, and I could hear myself breathe. I remember I just sat down and really appreciated the moment and noticed how comfy I was and how I could really hear myself think. I had forgotten what peace felt like. I even went further into peace mode and I meditated. I hadn't been this relaxed in years. I started to feel the energy flow in and out of my body; I started to feel the inner power that I had read and learned about. After the meditation, I put on my Bose speaker and blared "Mr. Jones" by the Counting Crows. The music just took over my body; I started to feel the rhythm, and I was enjoying the moment. For me, this moment was the key to unlocking the fun that I had inside me. I had forgotten what it felt like to have fun and to let loose. I had forgotten the feeling. Finding this feeling is an absolute key, because if you can feel it, you can duplicate it! Since then, I add fun into my day, every day, as I know, if you don't use it, you will lose it.

My advice to you is, take a day for yourself, a sick day, a holiday—hey, even if it's an unpaid day—to have a day just to yourself. You deserve it. Treat yourself. Find the feeling of letting loose, and think of everything you have ever wanted. Think of yourself right now, enjoying the freedom to do what you want, when you want. Appreciate it. The world is yours. Take it, give it back to the world, and enjoy it, and enjoy the process. Have fun with life, and life will have fun with you.

CHAPTER 7

QUESTIONS

What do I want you to get out of this chapter?

I want you to realize that you have all the answers you are looking for. The tricky part is asking the right questions. Did you know that your brain has to start looking for answers if you ask yourself a question? Only you know the answers that are best going to serve you. The goal of this chapter is for you to have an understanding of what questions you need to ask yourself on a daily basis to feel better, as feeling the best you have ever felt is the key to living a great life.

If you want to be a millionaire, if you want to be in the right relationship, if you want to lose weight, or maybe you just want to feel happier, all you have to do is ask the right questions to give you guidance. You may think that you have no idea on how to direct your focus, but you really do have all the power within you.

What do you mean I have all the power to give me the answers I am looking for?

What I mean by this is only you truly know what you need. We are all on our own journey to live life to its fullest. We all go at our own pace, and we all need different things, at different moments, to make ourselves happier. It's your guidance system that will steer you to what you want and need; you just have to allow yourself to receive the answers. In other words, it's your gut that will lead you to know if you're on the right page, as you can feel it. If you feel good, you know deep down that this is the direction in which you need to go. If you ask yourself a question and an answer comes to you that doesn't feel good, listen to your body, listen to your gut, as your actions and decisions should come with ease. If there is any resistance, it is a sign that you're not on the right path.

To prove that only you know the answers for you, can you think of a time when someone told you, "This is what you need to do!" Most of the time, you might think, "What does this person know? How do they know what I need to do? I am not doing that!" Or you might get defensive, as you realize that you know yourself best and that direction is not going to be pleasing for you.

Are you telling me that I should never ask for advice?

This is not what I am saying at all. There are many people from whom to seek advice. Usually the advice should come from people who have what you want. Be selective with whom you surround yourself.

Have you ever got advice about a relationship from a divorced friend? Have you ever got money advice from someone who is drowning in debt? Have you ever got advice from someone at work who is being unsuccessful? These are all things you would want to avoid.

I am still waiting to find out what you mean by I already know the answers

Here is a quick test. Ask yourself this question: What do I need, right now, to start feeling excited about life? Now sit there and listen to your mind. Your brain has to go to work on answering the question. The more relaxed and clear minded and in tune you are to yourself, the quicker the answers will start to flow in. Don't worry if the answers do not pop into your brain within the first five seconds; often the answers take time to flow in, depending on how quiet your brain is, and in most cases, there is so much noise going on it makes it hard to be in tune to any answers.

Have you ever tried to remember something that you were just talking about? Maybe it was the name of a movie or the name of an actor. You ask yourself, What movie was that actor in? You know the answer, but for the life of you, you can't think of the name. Hours or days later the name pops into your head out of nowhere. Answers can take time and come when you least expect them. Oftentimes, an answer will come to you in the middle of the night, when you are winding down, or simply lying there in bed, as this is when most people tend to be their most relaxed time of day.

Why is it so important I understand the power of asking questions?

Think of any problem you have in life. Recognize that you have the power to find a solution, and that your brain has to go to work and find an answer. Imagine having the confidence to solve any problem that you are faced with, as you know you already have the answers. All you have to do is ask the right question and be in tune with yourself to hear the answer. It's just a matter of time before you become ten feet tall and bullet-proof. Life can feel amazing once you start to feel unstoppable.

I still don't understand how I can have all the answers to all my problems

Here is the secret to this and what this book is all about. It's about feeling good, right now. One of the best ways to feel the best we have ever felt is to know that we have everything that we have ever wanted, we just have to come into alignment with it. This may sound hokey-pokey, but it's what all of the master teachers (such as Jesus, Buddha, Shakespeare, and Abraham Lincoln) have always talked about. You have all the abundance, love, joy, and happiness already inside you; your job is to let it out and circulate it back into the world. If you are not feeling good right now, then you are not connected to the feelings that are going to bring you the answers, as there will be too much resistance.

When you feel good, good things will start to happen, but only you will know what can make you feel good. The thought of feeling good can change from minute to minute, hour to hour, day to day. You will need different things at different times to bring you the feelings you are looking for.

When you ask yourself a question, your brain has to go to work on answering it. The kind of questions you should start to ask yourself are as follows: What do I need to do to feel a little bit better right now? Who do I need to connect with to bring a smile to my face? Where do I need to go to feel my best? Only you can answer these questions.

What if I am in debt and trying to become a millionaire?

Okay, first step, feel good NOW! This is always the first step. I say this because, not only will you start to attract good things/ people into your life, but when you're feeling good this is when the good thoughts start flowing to you. Have you ever been really stressed and tried to feel better, but you just can't as the stressful feelings are too hard to shake? For many, this is common as its very easy for the brain to think of worst-case scenarios. It will take time to dissolve these feelings by learning to appreciate the thoughts that we have. For now, try to feel a little bit better. If you're depressed, isn't it better to feel anger? This would mean you're moving in the right direction in the emotional scale.

Going back to the situation about being in debt, but wanting to be a millionaire, ask yourself what you need to do to feel good about money. There is a really good chance that if you're in debt or not in a great financial situation, when you think about money, you feel bad. When bills come in, you feel like you're drowning; when you spend money at the grocery store, you're stressing at the thought of your lack of money. If you're constantly feeling a lack of money, guess what, you are going to attract the opposite of abundance about money. Take the opportunity of being in debt as a positive, as it has brought you to this place of wanting abundance, and when you feel that you are abundant, you will attract abundance into your life. Ask yourself what thoughts of abundance feel like? What does my life look like when I am abundant? Repeat these questions as much as possible. Here is a tip, start your day off by questioning yourself on the feeling of abundance and what it looks like being a millionaire. These thoughts should feel good. It sets your mind right, and your brain will be searching for the good feeling thoughts all day. Another tip is to end the night off with these questions, as your brain will be working while you are sleeping. With enough repetition of these thoughts and questions, your brain will start to realize that you are living a millionaire's life. Once you have reprogrammed your brain, and you realize you are abundant, then you will attract abundance, as you are what you attract. So to find your greatness and find the good feeling thoughts, the answers and solutions will start to flow into your life faster than you can imagine.

Here is what will come out of this: at some point, answers will start to flow. Maybe you will get a million-dollar idea that pops into your head—who knows. Enjoy the magic of the universe, and know that good things are coming. Yes, it takes a level of trust, and yes, it takes a level of belief in yourself and the universe, but it is worth it. When you can fully surrender to the level of belief and trust in the feelings you feel, that is when the magic will show up in your life. One tip I have with all of this, is to learn patience. Things, people and ideas do not always come immediately, actually for the most part, things take time. Keeping faith and knowing things take time, do not rush things and do not doubt your thoughts. Stay consistent and every month or so, breakthroughs will happen. Trust me.

There is one thing about asking the right questions to trigger the right thoughts, you can ask any question, EXCEPT the HOW question. The moment you start to ask HOW, is the moment you start to disbelieve in your dreams. This disbelief will also get you to not feel good. If you are ever not feeling good about a situation, stop what you are doing and work on feeling good now. So for the HOW question, let the universe take care of this. You won't know the best and easiest path to reach your goals; just surrender to the universe, and only control what you can control, and that is feeling good now and focus on the end results and the feelings that will arise. (See chapters on belief)

What are some tips to make these things happen faster?

Things will come at the time you are ready. Have you ever heard the teacher will appear when the student is ready? The same thing applies. To get ready and be able to hear yourself, or in other words, to be in tune with your body, here are some tips that worked for me. Meditate 15 minutes every morning; start the day off with gratitude; be thankful for what you have. If you're in debt, but have a job, be thankful you have a job, be thankful for your comfy bed, be thankful for your TV. Be thankful for being here right now, reading this book, as you're getting better. Work out, let the serotonin kick in, and feel the stress relief. Read daily; constant growth should make you feel better. If you don't like reading, try audio discs.

It may take weeks or months to start to feel better, or it could happen right away; it depends on how busy your mind is. Here is the thing, if you don't have control over your mind, your mind has control over you! This could be the question: What do I need to quiet my mind? If you can't hear any answers, my suggestion would be to just breath, focus on your breathe, or Google learn to meditate. Do what works for you, and ask yourself what it is that you need to help you to speed up the manifestations. Only you have the answers.

Throughout this book, there will be many questions posed that stimulate thought. The purpose of this is for your brain to go to work, as we are all on our own journey to happiness, but only you will know what works for you.

What do you need to be great? Until the answer is nothing, as you are already great, you have some negative thoughts to release and you will need to develop some new thoughts to help you realize what you once were.

Be great, attract greatness!!

CHAPTER 8

EXERCISE

What do I want you to get out of this chapter?

This book is all about taking care of yourself first, and part of that is to move your body. Move your body on a regular basis. Take care of your body and your mind will follow. When you move your body, you will not only instantly start to feel better, but also decrease the stress in your life. Stress is the sole cause of anything wrong in our life. Stress is what puts our body out of alignment. The more stress we have, the harder it is to do things that will improve our life. When we are in a state of stress, it's signalling to our bodies that we are in a state of emergency; when we are in a state of emergency, we become in survival mode; and when we are in survival mode, we cannot open up our minds and our hearts to learn what is necessary to grow and expand to our potential.

Here is my story, some of which you already know: I grew up in an era watching Hulk Hogan. He was my idol. If you don't know who Hogan is, Google him. I wanted to be just like him. At an early age, I would ask my parents if certain foods, chips, for instance, were good for me; if they said no, I would not eat them. In my early childhood, I only ate good food. Actually, I can remember almost every dinner growing up there was a veggie, a meat, and potatoes. Looking at it now, we ate pretty boringly, but it was darn healthy, and it instilled some great eating habits in me. When I was eight, I got the Hulkamania Workout Set for my birthday. Hogan would be on the cassette saying, "Come on, Hulkamaniacs, you can do it, brother!" I remember doing push-ups and sit-ups and bicep curls almost every night.

My parents also worked out. My mom would bring us, on occasion, to her gym at the kids' club (I remember hating it!) My dad would blare the music and he would go downstairs in the basement and work out. I would sit on his feet while he would do sit-ups, and I would watch him sweat on his spinning bike. I was lucky because I had a great foundation already built.

The summer in which I was entering high school, I used my paper route money to purchase a gym membership. I would ride my bike 30 minutes across town to lift weights. I soon recruited a few of my buds to do the same thing. It became a thing that I just wanted to do: hang out with my buds and get jacked to be able to pick up girls. I remember after four months of this, and eating as much protein as I could, I noticed some serious gains.

I played soccer and golf at the early stages of working out. I became more confident on the field, and I felt like no one could compete with me; I knew I was one of the few putting in the work.

My golf game on the other hand went to crap. I had no idea that you should stretch after working out. My drives went from about 220 yards to 170, and I had developed a massive slice that lasted the whole season. Next season I started stretching and I was back to normal.

My workouts and sports continued through high school and university. After school, I decided to apply for a company called GoodLife Fitness. This is where I became a Manager Trainee, and my job was basically to sell gym memberships. This is when I realized the importance of adding fitness into your life. Fitness was very natural for me, but I was oblivious to the fact on how few people actually worked out. In fact, I found out that only about 20% of Canadians actually exercised in a gym; I was shocked to hear this. To me, this meant that people were living in constant stress. People were probably used to feeling stressed, low energy, moody, and had probably forgotten what it was even like to feel good.

I have spent the last 13 years surrounded by fitness professionals. I have seen it all, but it wasn't until recently that I felt what it was like to not work out.

It was Christmas break. I took two weeks off and I did not work out once. I was overeating, indulging in food and drinks. When January hit, we were swamped at work, and I only worked out once during the first week. The second week, I had a small procedure that prohibited me from working out for another ten days. This was the longest stretch I had gone without working out in my whole life. The week leading up to my ten days, I felt stressed for no apparent reason. Life was good, but I felt horrible. It's not like I gained too much weight or I was unhappy with how I looked; it was all the built up energy that was just stored in my body that I could not release. When the tenth day came, I did a spinning class and was able to release the energy. I felt great. The point is that I got to feel what people who don't work out feel day to day. The only difference is, I was aware of the drastic change in my life and how I felt, whereas if you have never worked out or haven't worked out for a while, you probably don't even know how bad you feel. Or you have become use to the feeling and don't even realize how good you could feel. This makes sense, though; it's not like you are going to feel change from day to day. It's like when you look in the mirror after working out: after the pump is gone, I bet you look like you did the day before. Change takes time, and how you feel takes time, but I challenge you that you can feel better if you start adding exercise to your routine.

Once you start to move your body, notice all the good changes that start to happen in your life. The release of stress will then allow you to release any resistance you have in your life. The less resistance you have, the more flow you have, and the more flow you have, this is when you start to let your desires be born.

What are the benefits of working out?

Read the book *Living the Good Life* by David Patchell-Evans, as he mentions over 125 benefits to exercising. Some benefits include improved sex drive, improved blood flow, slowing down the aging process, decreased stress, weight loss, muscle gain, glowing skin, and many more.

One of the greatest things about exercise is the immediate feelings you get. The release of endorphins, which combat stress, happens right away. After exercising, your neurotransmitters help release chemicals, such as serotonin and norepinephrine, which help make you feel good. They also help to combat stress. Higher levels of serotonin and norepinephrine ultimately make you feel good.

If you know anyone who has depression and is on medication, most likely their medication has serotonin and (or) norepinephrine to trigger their brain to make them feel better. Actually, everyone I have known with depression has been prescribed to work out.

Ultimately, you want to feel good. You are what you attract, and if you feel good, you will attract more good things into your life. Working out, moving your body, is one of the best things to get you to feel good right away. Not only will you work on the physical side, more importantly you will start to feel unstoppable as your confidence and self-esteem start to grow. You will start to realize how good you can actually feel.

Doctors say that 30 minutes on the treadmill is the equivalent to taking a Prozac and a Ritalin pill. Your body will release the chemicals to calm you, decrease your stress, and increase your focus.

In a society where there is more noise than ever, a society where many people are having hardships with relationships, their career (or lack thereof), where people are constantly on their phones, scrolling through social media, seeking strangers' approval, our bodies and minds need the ability to combat more stress, to feel a calmness, and to start feeling better.

Stress is where disease lives. The word disease is DIS-EASE, meaning not relaxed. All bad things happen in the form of stress. Earthquakes happen because of stress on the tectonic plates, cancer forms in the body because of cells under stress. If you're stressed or worried about something, this causes tension, which causes headaches. Your job then is to live a stress-free life, to allow you to be connected with your true self, as your true self is your most powerful, calm, and at-ease self.

So where do I start?

First off, get an image in your head of what you are looking to achieve, whether it's a new body or, even better, an image of how you want to feel. Next, make a decision to add exercise into your daily routine. The power of making a decision has enough energy to start to override any bad habit you may have.

Then find a place to work out. I recommend GoodLife Fitness if you're in Canada as GoodLife is a place with fitness professionals, and they have created a fun culture, full of caring associates who are ready to help out. Hire a trainer if you need the motivation or the knowledge to help you achieve your goal, or maybe you just need the accountability of having a trainer; either way, they are great. I have had many trainers in my life and I have always found that any investment I have put into myself, I have gotten back ten-fold. YOU ARE WORTH IT!

Join a group fitness class; my two favourites are yoga and cycling. The release of energy, the flexibility you will see, the increased energy, the fat loss, and the decrease of stress, just from these two classes will be amazing. Anything extra will be the cherry on top.

The key is to move your body. Release the endorphins and serotonin to feel good NOW.

What if I don't have time?

You will never find time. Life is busy. You need to make time. Your body and mind, combined, is the top priority. With working out, you will ultimately feel more confident, happier, and more at ease. What is more important? If you say your job or your family, I challenge this thought. Don't you think you would perform better at your job if you were more focused, had more energy, and felt better? Don't you think your family would benefit from you feeling better, even if it's just being a better role model for your kids? As a parent, I notice that I am a role model to my copycat kids who do and say exactly what I do. They are always watching. So isn't my goal to be the best I can be so they can see what greatness looks like, first hand?

No access to a gym? No worries. Go for a run, walk, do push-ups; there are a million exercise and workout clips on YouTube that you can follow along with. Today is the day that fitness becomes a top priority, as you deserve it for yourself. You deserve to feel your best.

Find that feeling that you're looking to feel; find that image of your body that you want to look like. What is life like feeling and looking your best? How would life be different? What would you be doing? What would you be wearing? Who would you be impacting? Repeat these visions and images in your head, day in and day out, and act daily until it becomes a part of you. The consistency of doing something over and over, not only creates a habit, but the habit becomes you. You are what you attract, so be strong, be fit, and be at ease.

If you just started to exercise, or if you have joined a gym before and only used it a handful of times, don't worry, it's not your fault. You weren't fully ready to make the changes. Change is a challenging thing to overcome. For the first month or two, it might seem tough, as you're not used to the lifestyle of exercising; that is why I encourage you to find a support system or hire a trainer. If you're paying for a trainer, you will show up.

More importantly, remember why you are doing what you are doing. Write it down. Create a vision board of what you want your new body to look like.

Finally, fall in love with feeling good. Enjoy the process. Enjoy the thought of being your best self, because if you feel great, you will attract greatness, and your life will start to change.

CHAPTER 9

THE POWER OF
MAKING A DECISION

What do I want you to get out of this chapter?

In this chapter, I will help you to understand the science of why making a decision is so powerful. Change starts to happen when you make a decision to want to change. The reason why most people don't make a decision is because they can't see how they are going to get to their destination. So what do they do? They keep doing things that they see how they can get there and that is why their life really never changes. o give an example, say I want to make a decision to become a millionaire, well most people don't make the decision to be a millionaire because they can not see how they are going to become a millionaire, so they continue making the same choices to make the same amount of money they know how to make. This is why I want you to decide what you want in life, even if you don't know how you are going to get there, just decide what you want in life, no limits....go.

I want you to decide that today is going to be a great day. I want you to decide that you live in abundance, and when I say abundance, I don't just mean financially, I also mean an abundance of love, gratitude, and joy. I want you to decide that feeling good right now, in this very moment, is the most important thing you can ever do. All of this starts with a decision. Decide to be great.

Going back about 13 years, when I was selling gym memberships, we had an add-on in which we sold start-up personal training. At the time, they were six, 30-minute sessions for $129 and twelve, 30-minute sessions for $229. I was always good at selling memberships, but not great at selling personal training. My general manager at the time (a great guy and a friend to this day) was always trying to figure out how I could get better at selling personal training. About three months went by and I was always finishing between 10% and 15% in personal training sales. In that third month, something clicked inside and I said to myself, that I was not going to let this happen again. I had an idea, and I told my general manager that I was going to sell starter packs of personal training. I had made a decision, and I was very clear on the decision, that I was going to sell personal training. It's not like I wasn't trying before, but this time I had made a decision that I was going to sell. Strange things started to happen. I felt more confident when I would present the packs. My flow was smooth, and I would get excited as I got to the point of educating the potential member about training. My sales went up to 40% that month on a high volume of sales. My paycheque increased substantially, and I led the division that month for total number of units. From that month on, I was in the top three (out of roughly 30 Fitness Advisers) for close to a year straight. The simple decision to sell personal training helped me get promoted to a general manager position, which I have now been in for the past 12 years.

The thing is, I didn't practice more, I didn't get any new piece of knowledge, there was no more incentive than usual to sell personal training, but when I made a decision, I realized that I had all the answers and that I could make this happen.

What's the science behind making a decision and why does this work?

We now have the science out there on measuring brain activity and the energy we give off at any given time. When you make a decision, and truly make a clear, decisive decision that change is necessary, the energy that is emitted is greater than the energy you are regularly emitting. In fact, it's so powerful that the energy in the decision is enough to start to reprogram your mind about what's possible. When this happens, new thoughts are born, which make it easier to start to create new habits, to bring more life to your goal. If you want to learn more about the science behind this, Dr. Joe Dispenza talks a lot about breaking old habits by making a decision. YouTube any of his stuff as he is a wealth of knowledge.

Making a decision is really the second step to achieving what you really want. Once you have a goal in mind, really commit yourself to the goal, and the energy that will start to flow will lead you to the answers that you are looking for. When I talk about commitment and going after a goal, you will have much, much more success if you really want what you're going after. If your only goal is only eight out of ten on the importance scale, then you're missing the point. If you commit, but not fully, the energy you give off will not be enough to break old habits to create new ones. It takes going all in to override your brain, to give you enough energy and focus to build the new habits it will take to find your success.

Test this out for yourself by really feeling the power in making a decision about something that you really want—just feel the energy start to flow. I want you to try, right now, to make a decision. Maybe you will decide that you are going to be filthy rich, or you will decide that today is going to be an amazing day. Whatever your decision is, really decide and commit to yourself. Commit to it as if you already know it's going to happen. What is it you truly desire? When you can bring yourself to believe in your decision, notice how you feel. Notice how powerful you can be, and notice any shift in your mindset from negative to positive. The power of making a decision for the better is an immediate shift of energy. It's literally like asking the universe for what you want, and by feeling the power of your decision, you immediately start to attract the tools/people/ideas into your life that will make your decision a reality.

Here is where it gets really interesting. Notice when you make a decision and when you really start to feel the energy flow. This decision is coming from a place from within. The goal is your desire that is wanting to be born from you. Listen to this, as it is key to everything that you want; if the desire is already inside of you, then that means you already have it. If it's already inside of you, that means it's already yours. You just have to let it go. So to know that you already have your goal is a powerful thing, because then you can start to "act as if."

Here is some more science and thoughts on making a decision

Most of our days are the same as the day before. It's said (proven) that 90% of our thoughts today are the same thoughts as yesterday. Thus if we are thinking the same thoughts that produce our actions, which result in who we are and what we get, then everything will always remain the same. If this is the case, then we are conditioning ourselves to reacting to our day. Our days become habitual. We are forming the habits to have the same feelings to produce the same actions that we perform, day in and day out, which ultimately determines the bulk of our character, of who we are. Now this is okay if you are 100% living your best life and you feel that you have no room for improvement or you're very satisfied with everything and have no desire to make any changes. This is your life and you will do what you want with it. I merely want to educate you that you have the ability to make changes from any circumstance you are in right now. However, if you're a believer that your thoughts control things (and I hope you do believe this), then our mission is to change our thought patterns and to develop new thoughts throughout the day that will benefit ourselves and our desires.

The opposite to reacting is to be proactive. If we are being proactive and deciding what we want our day/life to look like, then we are causing an effect, rather than reacting to the day. Our brains are merely a historical data safe that has a record of everything we have ever done; therefore, unless we are creating new thoughts, we will always be living in the past. The brain also does not know the difference between what has happened and what was imagined. So to create new thoughts, all we really have to do is decide on what we want, and imagine what life would be like when we have what we want. If we are focusing on what we want—also known as, the solution—rather than the problems, then all the answers will start flooding in. Done enough times, we start to become the thoughts, as we have conditioned our mind to develop the feelings, we need to attract our wants into our life. Thus, your ability to focus on what you want is key, so I ask you the question again, what is it that you truly desire?

When we decide on something we want, we are in the creative state. Here is a key point, though: when we decide on what we want, we have to imagine having it and becoming it, as opposed to we want this and that because we have a lack of this and that. If you think you need $100,000 because you don't have any money, then your attention is really on the lack thereof, and more lack will come into your life. It's VERY important to have the knowledge that your desire lives inside you (if it didn't, then you wouldn't be able to feel the desire, thus you already have it). When your wants in life come from a desire that is within you, then your thoughts come from a place of having instead of wanting, thus attracting more of who you are, which will get you what you want.

How will I know if I am coming from a place of having, compared to a place of wanting because I don't have?

The quick answer is, you will feel the difference. If you are ever feeling the lack thereof, the feeling won't feel good, but when you start to think that you already have something, you will really start to feel the abundance. There will be a big difference in how you will feel and you will know right away. The key to all of this is believing that you have everything you have ever wanted, believing that your desires live inside you waiting to be born. Without this belief ingrained in you, it will be difficult to come from a place of having. Here is another key part: if your desires already live inside you, all you have to do is let them be born. There is no development that you actually need, or no new ways to learn to achieve success, except learning how to become fully aligned with your goal. Once you become a vibrational match with your goal—meaning, once you 100% believe it's already yours—then all life will move mountains for you to manifest your goal into your life.

The cool thing is, once you start to imagine your goal and you are feeling the abundance and you are imagining what you want, as if you already have it, more of what you want will start to flow in. Momentum will pick up, and once it starts, it's a hard thing to bring yourself to a halt. I find that when momentum has built up, nothing will take you off track from your goal, and you become focused like you have never been focused before. I like to call it, you will have unleashed the beast from within! You will start to feel better and better, and ideas will pop into your head. If any idea runs into your head, trust your gut and roll with the desires, as each new desire or idea that pops into your head that feels good will lead you to a new breakthrough that will make you feel unstoppable.

What is the biggest struggle about the power of decision?

The biggest struggle that I had, and what I see from others, is making the time for yourself. Making the time to dream up your perfect day, your perfect life. You must want this in order to start to put conscious thought into your dreams. You also must believe that your thoughts become things. If you really believe this, then wouldn't you really want to start imagining your perfect day/life every day, and start to feel the excitement because you KNOW what's coming?

What if I don't believe that my thoughts turn into things?

My advice is try this out, but start small. Start to imagine something that you know you can receive, whether it is receiving a phone call from a friend who you haven't talked to in a while, or listening to a song that you really want to hear, or getting a new article of clothing that you want—something simple. Imagine yourself feeling good when you have what you want, and be patient. The more you imagine this as if you already have it, the quicker it will come into existence. Be patient, even forget about it for a couple days and be amazed when you get that phone call or get that new shirt, or your favourite song pops up on the radio at the most perfect time. Hopefully, the more you do this, the more confidence and evidence you will see in your life that thoughts do become things.

More about the struggles—be real with me

Not only do you have to make the time, but you have to start out by deciding on your dreams and by imagining your day. If you are not used to this, it will take practice. When I first started this process, I realized that I had not used the imaginative part of my brain for quite some time. If you don't use it, you lose it. I was slow at the start, but it gets easier with practice. Finding the time, before bed and in the morning, for this new habit to create is also tough. Schedule it in, and find enjoyment in the process, as if we don't, our lives will always be the same.

This process is like riding a bike: you will fall down, you will make mistakes, and you will lose focus. This is all okay, as it's part of the process. I am here to say it gets easier. A lot easier. You will start to be able to create automatically, and you will condition yourself to release anything that is holding you back from being able to let your life flow just like a river. Everything you want will start flowing to you if you just start to let go of control and believe that you already have what you want.

Your days will be more joyous than ever before. Stay with the process and soon you will start to see that your thoughts become things.

All of this starts with a decision, and then surrender your thoughts to the feelings of already having what you want. The ability to surrender to the universe and to have trust that the feelings you are looking for are coming is very powerful. You must be able to feel abundance before riches come into your life. You must feel love before love can come into your life. Decide on what you want and have faith that everything will start to come into your life. If it takes you a while to attach onto these feelings, this is okay. My advice to you is to keep on learning. Grab a book, meditate, listen to podcasts on self-development—this will start to give you more power and more of an understanding about realizing how much power you really do have. Or, trust what I am writing, as I am living what I am teaching, and I have found the answers that all great teachers have taught before. The answers are here for you. This could be the only book you ever read, to know that the secret to life really does lie within.

Remember, faith is trusting the understanding of how the universe works, which vibration precedes manifestation. The Law of Attraction states that whatever you think about wants you, just remember to combine the law of attraction with the law of emergence. Come from a place of having instead of wanting because you don't have, then the law of attraction will go to work for you. It has to, it's a universal law!

So where do I start?

Start right now, and make a decision of what you really want in life. Start first thing in the morning, and this will set the tone for the day. It is a lot easier to go with momentum, and if you start your day off with a positive mindset, the momentum will continue. If you start by doing the same thing you normally do, your day will start in the past, and the same old things will show up in your day.

Start by saying, Today is going to be a great day; I don't know what is going to happen, but I know that good things are flowing my way. Now you are setting an intention and making a decision to live your best life.

I say, decide to be great! Feel great, attract greatness.

CHAPTER 10

FEEL YOUR WAY TO SUCCESS

What do I want you to get out of this chapter?

Believe it or not, you are 100% in control of your thoughts, and your thoughts are directly related to how you feel. Therefore, the only thing stopping you from feeling total bliss is all the thoughts that you have been creating to make up your belief system. You are your worst enemy; at the same time, you are your greatest ally. The great thing is, we do have a choice regarding our thoughts, which will result in how we feel. With this knowledge, I want you to choose and commit to feeling pure love/abundance/appreciation/excitement and pure happiness, all the time. There is literally no better thing in life then feeling good NOW. Once you feel like you have everything, you then need nothing, which is when you actually get everything.

So where do I start?

First, I want you to know that there are many different emotions, and wherever you are on your emotional scale is okay. At the top of your emotional scale are pure love, abundance, appreciation, bliss. Down from there are passion, eagerness, happiness, hopefulness, and contentment. Some emotions that start heading toward feeling not-so great are frustration, worry, rage, jealousy, hatred, insecurity, guilty, depressed and the worst feeling, in my opinion, of all is powerless.

Even though the ultimate goal is to feel pure love/appreciation, if you are at the bottom of the scale, feeling depressed/powerless/insecure/guilt, the goal is to feel a little bit better, each day, each hour, minute to minute. Always progress yourself to feel better, as your feelings will act like a magnet and attract more of those feelings towards you. If you're feeling anger, that's better than feeling depressed. Regardless of where you are at emotionally, if you want to attract more of what you want, then feeling better is the key. So, how do you feel right now? Are you feeling powerful and confident? Are you feeling contentment or are you feeling depressed? Take a couple of seconds to really notice how you are feeling, and know whatever you are feeling, its ok.

Depending where you are on the journey, it might take a little bit, but step by step, *paying attention* to your feelings and quieting your mind will start to work your way up the emotional scale.

FEEL GREAT, ATTRACT GREATNESS

It's true, time heals. It's also true that you are in the perfect place at this exact moment, as whatever is going on in your life, your current situation is teaching you and bringing you to a spot where you can learn to let go and let the goodness soak in. Many times, you might not be able to see the light at the end of the tunnel. That's okay, just know that you are on a path to live in extreme happiness and appreciation. An easy way to put yourself in a better situation is to imagine a worse-off situation. Just imagine for a moment that you live in a Third World country where finding clean water would be the best feeling in the world. Imagine, you celebrated when it rained and you danced when you knew your crops would have a chance to grow. Imagine sleeping on an old potato bag, as this is the only thing for comfort.

Now, take a look around. If you're reading this and you live in North America, realize you have already won the lottery. You truly do have it all. You have the necessities in life, and most likely, you are living in comfort. Everything else that's coming or that you have is just gravy.

Maybe a not-so-good situation will teach you appreciation when you get through it. A life living in appreciation is a life in which great things happen. I challenge you to appreciate the pain, as the pain will bring you closer to understanding your greatness. When you learn to appreciate, there is no resistance; when there is no resistance, there are only pure good feelings. These pure good feelings can't be described. Once you get there, you know what I am talking about, as you will be able to feel the power from within.

A pure moment

I want to share a pure joy/love moment with you. When I was 32, I had my daughter. The moment the doctor brought her out and I saw her face, I said, "She's beautiful" and I cried uncontrollably. The tears were flowing. This was the first time in my life where the feeling of love had completely taken over my body and my mind to the point where tears were coming down and all I could feel was pure love. It was one of the purest feelings I have ever felt. I remember even laughing because I couldn't stop the tears. I had fully let the love in, and euphoria took over.

Have you ever got to this point? When was the last time you have fully released and let in the good feelings? And, no, I am not talking about sex—that's something different.

Are you saying that you can get to the point of pure LOVE to the point where tears are flowing whenever I want?

I am saying that these thoughts are feelings that are there for you whenever you want. All you have to do is tune into the right frequency to allow the thoughts to bring out the good feelings. Look at it this way, electricity is everywhere, but if you're not plugged in, there is no charge. One way to do this is to ask for the feeling. Try this, ask yourself to feel more appreciation or more love or more abundance. Instantly, you start to focus on these feelings, and these good feelings start to come in. (This might not work if you are too far down on the emotional scale; in this case, ask for a closer feeling to where you are.) Energy flows where attention goes, and it happens instantly.

Another way to go get the feeling is to relax. I personally meditate, but I recommend that you find the best way you know how to relax, preferably without drugs or alcohol, which only serve as a bandage. It is better to develop the ability to relax without substances; to develop the knowledge that you can ease your mind with your abilities is a more powerful tool. Once you are in a spot where you can totally relax, you start to let go of all the negative thoughts and open yourself up to better feeling thoughts. Eventually, you will not have to think of any thoughts and you will just be in the flow of life itself. Even with the thought of letting go, you can start to notice that you feel better. If you can notice that you are feeling lighter and a little bit better, appreciate that feeling, and notice how relaxed and how good you feel. I always say, you don't realize how crappy you feel, until you start to feel good. Pay attention to how good you feel when you are in an appreciative state, and you will more easily be able to attract these feelings on a day-to-day basis.

Here is a quick story about another way to create better feeling thoughts and feelings. On February 13th every year, I give my daughter a rose and we go out on a date night (thank you, Garry, for this idea). We dress up to the nines—I will be in a suit and she is usually in a princess dress—and we will go out to our local restraunt. This year, I felt she was old enough that I could write her a note about ten things that I love about her. I thought this would make her smile. So I start writing, and I noticed that I had a big smile on my face. I was thinking about how amazing my daughter is and how proud I am of her. All these thoughts and feelings of love started pouring in. I tell you, I got so much out of it, I didn't want to stop. I actually didn't; I then started to write ten things that I love about my wife. These love thoughts and feelings continued for a long time afterwards.

If we put effort into a thought, the Law of Attraction states that more of those thoughts will come about. Like attracts like. Also, as I mentioned before, by writing things down, there are 10,000 connections between your hand and brain, and this helps to create those neural pathways that you truly desire. It's easier said than done as, it takes effort to make the time. Do what you have to do to make time for yourself, and think about what makes you feel good, as more good will come flowing into our life like never before.

What if I try to think good thoughts,
but all these negative thoughts keep on
interrupting my desired thoughts?

Many of us have been conditioned and have created the habit of thinking and feeling in terms of the worst-case scenario. The good part about where you are right now with these thoughts is that you're probably at a point where you're sick and tired of being sick and tired. When you get to this point, you want more than ever to feel good. When all you want is to feel good, that is when you put more effort and thought into getting better in your situation. It's like being the short stack at the poker table: you're either going to fold or go all in. No one can bluff you out of the pot; you're all in.

Here is a quick story, about a professor and a student, to better demonstrate my point. The student really wanted to be successful and filthy rich. The professor brought the student to a lake and held the student's head down in the water. He held his head down until the student was about to die. When the student's head popped up, he asked the teacher, "Why did you do that?" And the professor asked, "When you were under water, what is that you wanted?" The student responded, "To breathe." The teacher then said, "When you want to be successful as bad as you want to breathe, then you will be successful." The moral of the story is you really must want to feel better. If you kind of want to feel better, you will get mediocre results.

What will I have to overcome to achieve the ultimate feelings?

One tricky part that you will have to overcome is the bad habit thoughts you have already created. My advice, and what has worked for me, and countless other people, is meditating. Meditating will help you not only release negative thoughts, but also rebuild yourself into the person you want to become.

I recommend that you research the benefits of meditating and (or) download the CALM app and start immediately. Meditation is like weeding a garden and the garden is your brain. The more you weed, the clearer and more beautiful the garden becomes. When you're left with no weeds, there are only good thoughts to be had, and your garden will flourish.

The toughest part about practising meditation is making the time. The question that I have for you is, what is more important than feeling good right now? What more could you want for yourself than feeling good? Treat yourself as a top priority and make time for YOU! Even if it's waking up an hour earlier every day. You won't regret it!

What else can I do to move up the emotional ladder?

Start to develop an attitude of gratitude. Start and end each day with what you are grateful for. Starting your day like this will build a positive momentum to your day. Momentum is a tough thing to stop: once it's big enough, you become a bull running full-steam ahead. Imagine yourself as if you were a sports team that is dominating: your offense is clicking, your defence is creating turnovers; you feel unstoppable with momentum on your side. Your momentum builds up strong enough that you become the most dominant team in the league, or even better, the most dominant team in history, as everything you plan on comes to fruition.

It's also helpful to end the night off in gratitude. You will notice that your last thoughts are similar to your first thoughts in the day. Also, your brain doesn't sleep, so maximize those eight hours when you are resting to allow your brain to go to work for you.

The fastest way to get what you want and to feel good is to appreciate what you have. If you constantly think about having no money, start to think about what you have: your house, your car, your job, and maybe the clothes on your back and the food in your fridge. Money has always shown up when you have needed it, and, guess what, it will this time; you just have to appreciate money and it will flow. (I'll talk more about this in the upcoming chapter on money.)

When I first learned about meditating and appreciating, I remember that right after I meditated I would journal. And before I started writing, I remember looking up and seeing everything I had—a beautiful house, my health—and I saw pictures of my family on the wall. It was at that moment that tears started to come down, and I realized I had everything I had ever wanted. I realized, I have everything and I need nothing. Life is good.

Side note: I am not a crier. These are some of the rare occasions that I have cried. Although, I do wish I did cry more, as it has been pure feelings of joy and love that have taken over my body. That pure feeling is priceless.

Final thoughts

To move up the emotional ladder and start to feel the success, the appreciation, the love, and the abundance to attract more of that feeling into your life, you must want to feel good. To bring more attention to your feelings, you must start to notice how you are feeling. When you start to become aware of your thoughts, you will start to live more in the present moment. So I challenge you to want to feel better than you have ever felt before and to search for a better thought feeling, as you will start to live a life you want to live. It will be a life in which you are waking up with excitement because you can't wait for all of the exciting things that are going to show up or happen to you today.

There is nothing more important than feeling good right now. The sooner you can understand this, the sooner your life will change for the better. You have the power: feel great, attract greatness.

CHAPTER 11

MONEY

What do I want you to get out of this chapter?

You have the power to create any riches you want in life. How much do you believe you're worth? Whatever you can imagine, and bring yourself to believe, is what you will achieve. Money, like everything else, is energy. At the end of this chapter, I hope you will have an increased belief and awareness about your power to not only attract money into your life but also to realize how abundant you really are.

I have read over a dozen books about money, including *Think and Grow Rich* by Napoleon Hill, *The Wealthy Barber* and *The Wealthy Barber Returns* by David Chilton, *Acres of Diamonds* by Russell H. Conwell, *Rich Dad Poor Dad* by Robert Kiyosaki and Sharon Lechter, *Secrets of the Millionaire Mind* by T. Harv Eker, and many more. They all have different and important messages, but the one message that has popped up over and over again is how we think and feel about money. The way we think has the ultimate effect on our relationship with money, which in turn determines how much we are worth.

So many of us desire to have riches, but many of us lack the riches we desire—why is this? Whether you believe it or not, the sole reason for riches is how we feel about money. Money, like everything else in this world, is energy. Any scientist, or any master teacher in the world, will tell you this. So the secret to having all money, according to the Law of Attraction is to feel good about money. When you feel good about money, you are in alignment with money, and you will allow the money to flow to you. The reality is, most of us do not feel good about money. When we think about money, we are actually creating further separation because our thoughts are coming from a place of want, instead of a place of having. I have experienced this first hand—wanting and thinking I loved money so much, but, as I became more aware of my thoughts and feelings, I noticed that all my thoughts towards money were actually coming from a place of wanting. A place of wanting is the same as coming from a place of lack, thus it created a further lack of money in my life. It wasn't until I learned to come from a place of having that money started to flow into my life.

Some key secrets

The first secret I have for you is to be aware of your thoughts about money. You might be thinking that you love money and that you 100% feel good about money, but I challenge this thought. I, too, thought that I loved money, but what I realized was, whenever a bill came in, I felt frustrated instead of thankful for the service. Whenever I went out to spend money, I felt bad, as I had the thought that I only had a limited amount of money. These thoughts were self-limiting and actually made me feel stressed and put me in a not-so-good mood. The challenge that I have for you is to pay attention to how you feel when you spend money. When you get bills in the mail, really notice what thoughts you have. A great book that will help you change the money blueprint in your mind is *Secrets of the Millionaire Mind: Mastering the Inner Game of Wealth* by T. Harv Eker.

The next secret would be to pick an amount of money that you believe you could achieve. The key word is believe. I want to say it's as easy for you to attract one dollar into your life as it is attract one million dollars. When you can bring yourself into full alignment with your belief of already having this money, the money will come rushing into existence. Now, you might be thinking, "Yeah, right!" Again, it's not just me who is saying this; this is what all the master teachers have been saying. The key to believing is understanding the Law of Emergence, which means you already have everything inside you. You are, and have, an infinite abundance, as you are connected with source energy. Once you can fully believe and understand the Law of Emergence, a flow of abundance will take over your body and money and (or) opportunities to make money will start to appear in your life. Just like the Law of Emergence talks about, the acorn already has the oak tree from within; the acorn does not have to attract the oak tree, it just has to let the oak tree out and it does so by allowing the right conditions to create it. Unlike an acorn, which is indigenous, we are endogenous, meaning, we carry, and we can create, our own conditions. Therefore, once we can allow the belief to achieve whatever money we desire, we can allow the money to flow itself into manifestation. Another way we can start to increase the belief and come into alignment is to start and end our day off by envisioning ourselves and what it would be like to live life with an amount of riches. If these imaginations feel good, then you're on the right track, and over time, the repetitions from the imaginations will have ingrained deep neural pathways and feelings that become you. Remember, you are what you attract.

Another secret I have is to pay attention to your money. Energy flows where attention goes. The word currency means flow; the word affluent means flow. These are signs that you have to let the money flow to you. Here is a story demonstrating this thought. When my wife and I had bought our first house, we had to get the house furnished. We went to The Brick and bought our king-size bed, couches, multiple TVs, and spent $16,000 on our Brick credit card. At the time, we thought, no problem—my brother was living with us—we will put his rent money every month towards the credit. That didn't happen! Actually, for the next three years, we put roughly $100 per month on the card—until we looked at how much we owed three years later—and we still owed $16,000. This was when we started to set a goal to become debt free, and we created a thermometer, visually showing us our progress in paying off our credit card. The thermometer had the amount of $16,000 at the top, and we coloured the chart every week, when we put money towards our debt. We had decided that before we had kids we wanted to be debt free. We found joy in paying off the card, as we felt accomplished. Exactly one year later, we paid off the card. We were putting anywhere from $1,000 to $2,000 every month onto the card. We went from paying $100 a month to, on average, magically, paying off $1,500 per month. To this day, I have no idea how we easily found the money; it sort of just happened. Funny thing was, we set a reward for ourselves that once we paid off our card, we'd go out and have a nice night out in Niagara Falls. Sure enough, we had an amazing dinner, and we started dreaming about how we were going to spend an extra $1,500 per month that we had magically found. The next day, we found out we were having a baby. We said, scrap all the plans we made last night.

Another key to attracting abundance is the power of giving away abundance. There is something magical about spending money on someone else that makes you feel good. The more you can give away your abundance in a manner that makes you feel good, the more abundance will start to flow. By giving away abundance, it strengthens your belief that you are abundant. You are what you attract, so build yourself up to be the most abundant person you can be.

The last spiritual tip I would have on the topic of money is to be grateful for it. Remember, if money is energy and we are what we attract, then our relationship with money must be one of pure love, to let the energy flow into our lives. The best way to immediately start to feel good about money is to be grateful for what you have. Instantly, your thoughts and feelings become more positive towards abundance. When bills come in, feel grateful for the service that you are receiving. When you spend money, think about the joy from the purchase and be thankful for the convenience, as most parts of the world do not have organized grocery stores, clothing stores, technology stores, and so on.

So all I need to do is feel good about money and believe I have it and it will come?

Technically speaking, yes, but here is the thing, when you're in alignment with your belief in abundance, then people, ideas, and opportunities will start to attract you. You will be required to take action, and the action will feel good. Part of the action might be having a tool to create the money you desire.

If you are $10,000 in debt and making $30,000 per year and only have enough money to live, having another source of income is necessary. Ideas, such as a network marketing company, investments, or some other tool to have your money working for you, will be required.

*What if I just don't have enough money to live and
pay off debts when my side business isn't working?*

This is where many people live. I see it in their faces—the stress
about money—I hear it in their words; they physically don't
have enough money. I'll bring it back to my first point: you
need to learn to feel good about money. More than ever, you
need to start to learn to feel good about money and to believe
that you are abundant. Carol S. Dweck has a great book called
Mindset. This book talks about a fixed mindset versus a growth
mindset. With a fixed mindset, you believe that you don't have
control and things are the way they are. With a growth mindset,
you believe that you have the power in every situation. More
than ever, you will be required to have a growth mindset to
start to believe that you have everything you need. As long as
there is resistance, money cannot flow into your existence.

*What are some things I can do to make the shift from
thinking of lack of money to pure abundance?*

There are a few things you can do right away. The first thing,
and the quickest way to feel more abundant, is to be grateful for what you already have. I'm thankful for all the money
coming in, I'm thankful for my investments, I'm thankful that
I have enough money for food, I'm thankful for the bills that
provide me to live in comfort, I'm thankful for the roof over my
head, I'm thankful for my car and having enough gas to get to
work. Here is the kicker: be grateful for your current situation,

even if you do feel like you're drowning in debt, be grateful for where you are, as a couple things will start to happen. The more you can give awareness/appreciation to your situation, the more bad feelings will start to fade. Also, maybe you were meant to have these feelings to learn how to get better at your thoughts towards abundance. What is that saying, give a man a fish and you feed him for a day; teach a man to fish and you feed him for a lifetime. I appreciate this journey about learning to feel abundance. It's worth it!

Another thing I would do is pick up a book about money. I would personally start with *Think and Grow Rich*, as I have felt it to be one of the most accurate books out there. Try to read a book a month about money. This will help you keep your focus on what you want to attract. Remember, energy flows where attention goes.

Another thing I've talked about throughout this book is meditation. Meditating will help you to release your negative thoughts about money, and it will allow you to develop new thoughts. Here's an example: maybe you are thinking that money only comes with hard work and it comes in two times per month. What if you had the thought that money comes easily and frequently, and you really had this ingrained in your soul? How would you feel about money knowing this? Scrap any thought you had about money and realize the universe is at your command, and if you desire abundance, and believe you are abundant, abundance will flow.

Lastly, I want you to forget about the money and do more of what you love. This might be hard to understand, but I have learned this the best through a short YouTube video by Alan Watts called, *What If Money Was No Object?* Watch this video, as there is undeniable truth in it. It talks about doing what you love and the money will come.

Forgetting about the money and doing what you love is part of the main message in my book, which is, feeling good now. If all you did was focus on feeling good, then you would not be feeling lack and creating further separation, instead your feelings of love and abundance and letting everything that you desire (including money) would flow into your existence. As weird as this may sound, the universe knows what you want. All you have to do is feel good, as this is the key; this is always your main objective, as you are what you attract.

Become abundant in your mind before you physically have the abundance, it will then allow you to feel the abundance, which will attract abundance to you.

Feel abundant, attract abundance.

CHAPTER 12

FLOW

What do I want you to get out of this chapter?

I want you to understand that life is happening for you, not against you. Once you are in the flow of things, you will realize that life is great. Finding your flow, and being in the flow, is a goal that I believe we should all strive towards, because when you are in the flow, you have everything and you need nothing. You can feel the appreciation as life slows down and you perform at your best. This is when you can't be stopped. Everything is going your way. You have no thoughts in your mind, as you're only focused on the present moment. It's a beautiful thing, and I challenge you to find your flow more often.

*So is life happening regardless of flow? Why
is it important to reach this state?*

When you are in the state of flow, desired outcomes tend to
happen. Time flies by because you're enjoying the moment.
You feel a sense of ease and a sense of knowing. When you
aren't in a state of flow, there is some sort of resistance happening, whether it's a negative thought or a negative belief that is
holding you back from complete potential.

Here's a story about Mickey Mantle and Ted Williams about
why it is important to get into the flow. First off, if you don't
know who Mickey Mantle and Ted Williams are, they were
two of the best baseball players, arguably of all time. Mickey
Mantle was known for being one of the best batters of his time,
and he was also a switch hitter, which was a rarity back then.
Teddy Williams, was a phenomenal ball player, an all-star, and
he was known for being a student of the game, as he loved
understanding the mechanics of the swing. Teddy was one of
the first guys to understand that you didn't need to have a heavy
bat in order to hit the ball farther. It was all about being able
to maximize the speed of your swing. Regardless, Ted Williams
and Mickey Mantle were chatting in the outfield in an All-Star
Game. Teddy was fascinated with Mickey, as he was not only
a great ball striker but also a switch hitter. Teddy was asking
Mickey questions like, "What eye do you see the ball coming
out of? When do you notice the ball coming out of the pitch-
ers hand? When do you get prepared to swing?" After all the
questions, Mickey wasn't really sure of the answers, as he was

used to just swinging the bat. After the All-Star Game, Mantle went on the worst hitting slump of his career, as he was putting more thought into his swing. Every little mechanical question Teddy asked made Mickey really think about his swing . It wasn't until Mickey was able to let go of the questions and thoughts and just swing that he was able to get back on track to his great career.

This is a story about letting go of control, for when we try to control, our mind gets in the way. Let go and find the natural flow and let the magic begin.

If you're a golfer, you might have seen or experienced this for yourself. The longer you think about your shot and try to remember what you need to do for your swing, the more likely you are to duff the ball. My message: grip it and rip it!

In the movie, *Tin Cup* (and if you haven't seen it, I highly recommend it), when Kevin Costner has a case of the shanks, and uses every tool and gadget he has to hit the ball, he still can't get rid of his bad shots. It isn't until his caddie makes him look like a fool that Kevin starts to hit the ball straight. What the caddie had done was, he took the focus off hitting the ball and put the focus on Kevin looking life a fool. This made Kevin let go of trying to control his swing. Let go; surrender, as life is going to happen, and watch the good things roll into your life.

So how do I let go and get into the flow?

It seems like I'm repeating myself, but meditation is the best answer I know. Listen to your breathing and be in the present moment. The more you meditate, the easier it will be to learn to let go and release all the negative thoughts from holding you back. Also, meditation will help as you will start to get used to the feeling of being relaxed, and as your mind takes over your body will follow. Studies prove that the more you meditate, the easier it will be to get into a state of flow on a regular basis.

Life is happening regardless of whether you are in the flow. The Law of Attraction is always working, regardless of whether you believe or know about the law. The same goes for the Law of Emergence. Try this: focus on your breathing. You can notice yourself breathing; regardless of whether you lose focus, you will still be breathing. When you are focusing on breathing in and breathing out, you're controlling your breath. When you're not controlling your breath, you're still breathing. Life is the same way. Let life happen to you because it is going to happen regardless. Just let go and surrender to knowing that things always work out! Let go of your stress, let go of your worries, let go of any past problem; be in the present moment and enjoy life, as life is happening for you, as you will always get what you've always wanted. Whatever you have wanted is coming, rushing into your existence, you just have to allow it. When you are trying to control life and how it goes, this is when we make mistakes and life feels hard. This is when what we desire will take a long time to manifest itself into your life. Can you think of a time where things have gone your way perfectly, better than you could have imagined? Can you think of a time where everything has slowed down and you felt like you could not make a mistake? This is the state of flow I am talking about.

To get into the flow is being present and being aware of your current situation. The focus you will have when you are truly in the flow will be the most focused you have ever encountered in your life. It's like a laser beam of intense focus, and you can start to pinpoint your next steps. You will find the path of least resistance to make you happy. Life will be easy. Have ever heard the saying, "If it's hard, you're doing it wrong"? Hopefully this chapter will give you more of an understanding of that saying. Life should be easy, it should be free-flowing, and it should be fun. Side note: the times when things feel hard are the times when you're learning a new skill and creating a new habit. These times take effort, as your old thought patterns will pop up and you will have to challenge yourself to stay course. The old thought patterns will feel comfortable, as you have been used to them; so challenge yourself to stay focused on what you truly want. The more you find yourself building the habits to create success, the easier it will be for you to find your flow.

If you listen to any top athletes and you hear stories about how they helped win the big game, you will notice a pattern of success. Time and time again, you hear things like the moment just slows down, they knew exactly what move to make, what pitch to throw, what shot to take, what punch to throw—they were just in the zone!

Go back to the chapter on having fun (Chapter 6). This will also help you to have an understanding that having fun is when you're feeling good. I had the pleasure of interviewing the number 2 and 4 prospect in the world for football, Evan and Noah Clarke. Evan a QB and Noah a RB, both dominant Canadian football players, one day possibly seeing them in the NFL, they both said, "when they get in the zone, they were just playing the game and having fun". Their moves became effortless! The feeling you're searching for is effortless, or in other words, you feel at ease.

The more you can be in the zone is the moment your desires will flow into existence. Find your flow by releasing your thoughts through meditation, practice your habits, and most importantly, have fun, as everything you want is rushing towards you. Know this, appreciate this, and surrender to all the hard work you have put in to get to this point and the flow will be yours. You are in the perfect place at the perfect time to have everything you have ever wanted. Appreciate this moment, and feel effortless to attract effortless.

CHAPTER 13

ACTION

What do I want you to get out of this chapter?

Nothing will come to you without action. There is a story about a man who really wants to win the lottery. He has had a terrible year: he has lost his job, he is forced to take a second mortgage on his house, he is loaded with credit card debt, his financial situation has driven him to depression. His life is spiralling out of control. The man feels hopeless, and he feels he truly needs a miracle to help him out of this hole.

With nowhere else to turn, this man decides to pray to God: "Dear God, please help me with the lottery. I really need the money. Please, help me!"

After weeks of praying and no results, this man prays for something different. "All right, God, I've asked you countless times, but it really seems like you aren't listening to me. I've asked you to help me win the lottery, but still I haven't won. Are you even listening?"

What happens next truly shocks the man. He hears a voice; God speaks from above: "Buy a lottery ticket, you fool!!"

You can ask for what you want, but if there is no action, the result will not come.

Here's the thing, once you get your thoughts right and get clear on what you want, you will want to do the actions. Actions will come with ease and enjoyment, and they will make you feel good.

Remember that your thoughts control your emotions, which lead to how you act, which in turn help you become who you want to be and get what you want to have.

What if I hate doing what I am doing or my actions feel like a struggle?

This is a clear indicator that you're not in the sweet spot. If it feels hard and you don't enjoy what you're doing, my advice to you is, please stop and start to get clear again on what you want. You might be reading this and thinking, yeah, right, just stop, life is supposed to be hard, losing weight is supposed to be tough, making money is all about the grind, nothing comes easy, I deserve to go through the struggle.

I can see how you might be thinking these things as I once had many of these thoughts—until I started to change my beliefs, then everything started to come with ease. There is good with your struggle and hardship, though, as right now you are in the perfect spot where you need to be to catapult your life to where you want to go.

Oftentimes, it's our struggle that helps us get clarity on what we really want, and once we know exactly what we want, we can start to surrender to the universe as life will guide us to the actions we need to take to achieve our dreams. This might be hard to understand, as it takes faith/believing in your goals, understanding that your thoughts are vibrations, and everything in this world is a vibration, which means we are all connected in some way. Watch *What the Bleep Do We Know!?* It's about the quantum physics of this world. Even the top scientists that study quantum physics cannot fully explain how it works, but it might give you a little understanding on how life can flow to you once you get your thoughts in line with your vision.

Regardless, you don't need to know how it works; all you need to do is to get clear on what you want; believe that you will get it and the right actions will come to you.

How will I know if I am doing the right actions?

The actions will feel good, plain, and simple. You will be excited to do the actions, as you know that you are moving closer to your goal. Here are a couple of examples. As I'm writing this book, it's 4:30 a.m. and I am so happy and excited to be up this early. Also, if you know me, I wasn't always an early riser, as, like many, I enjoy my sleep. I really enjoy my sleep. I make sure I always get a minimum of nine hours at night. Sleep to me is like gold, so for me to get five hours of sleep, to be up writing my book, not to mention I was actually up at 3:30

meditating, there has to be a good reason. Why? Because I love my actions and I love feeling good. For me, working on myself and having my alone time before the kids awake is priceless.

Here is an example to help you understand the love for action

I'm a big football fan. For you, think of any professional sports athlete and their journey to success—what would it take? Any professional football player who plays in the National Football League has such a passion and love for the game. They have most likely been playing since they were a kid, setting records at high school, and really starting to mature into NFL talent in college. There are early mornings and late nights of practicing, playing, going through game footage. Where am I going with this? People may look at the path of a pro athlete and could never dream of how much work it took for these individuals to get where they currently are. In fact, people would get scared of all the "hard work" it took. Here's the thing, you talk with any of these athletes or watch any of their life stories/documentaries, and yes, it took work and effort but the love for their goal to make it into the NFL took over their bodies and minds. They all found enjoyment in the process. The focus and vision top athletes have on their goal, propelled them to do the things that most people find hard. So what's hard to many, becomes a sense of pleasure as a love for the game, and a love for the vision takes over.

When you first start something, a hundred percent of the time it will take effort and will feel tough, but it will feel rewarding.

It doesn't matter how far you need to go or how big your dream is, by focusing on your end goal, instead of all the problems or tough tasks ahead, you'll find a sense of ease toward actions. The actions become the pleasure, and in turn you will want to do more of those actions, until a point comes where you only think about the actions, as you are getting such a great pleasure or a great reward. Becoming obsessed with your goal: this is the ultimate focus.

I want you to think back to something you love or once loved. For me, it's golf. In high school, I would deliver papers at 5:00 a.m. and be at the golf course for 6:30 a.m. I would play two rounds a day, 120 rounds in the summer, and if you know anything about golf, that's a lot of hours at the golf course. Needless to say, I am pretty good at golf, too—by no means a pro, but chances are, I could take you in a round. Did I look at golf as a chore for getting good? Not at all! I truly enjoyed every minute of it.

Here is a hint question: Have you ever loved performing a task so much that time went by so fast? If so, what was it, and how can you find time to do more of that?

What if I don't do anything but party with friends or just chill and watch Netflix?

This is a great question, as I feel many people would be thinking this way. I would say if this is truly all you want to do, find a vehicle to make this happen. Start a business to help create the time and money and freedom to make this a reality. Use the vision of freedom and relaxing to propel your actions. Just think of how many people are making millions these days by doing pranks and posting them to YouTube. Take all the young millionaires out there doing network marketing business. The way of the future is changing. Whatever you want, and bring yourself to believe, you can achieve.

What if I don't want to start any business and don't have any skills that people would want?

My advice is, fall in love with self-development. The process of getting to know yourself leads to the highest gifts you will ever receive. When you can truly know and love yourself, you will feel like you have everything and you will then need nothing. When you can get to the spot in your life where you know that everything that you have ever desired lives inside you, that will be the moment when your desires start to manifest themselves into your life faster than you could ever imagine. Life becomes your catalogue for whatever you want, and you become more free and grateful than you have ever become. Picture the best version of yourself. What does this look like? How will you show up to life?

Here are a couple tips to get started on enjoying the actions and letting the actions come to you

First off, discover what you want. The more you visualize what you want, the more you program your subconscious mind to attract what it needs. A great tool for this is a vision board.

Start with small actions. If you're going to the gym, start off by just showing up, maybe walk on the treadmill, use light weights, make it easy and do not kill yourself. When I first started to read and dive into self-development, I started reading one page per day. Then it becomes two pages, then a chapter; it all starts with doing something each day. Consistency is key, as it helps keep the focus!

Next, start your day off with action. It builds momentum for the day. Momentum is a powerful thing. Wake up a bit earlier, go for a run, read a page of a book, meditate for 15 minutes— just do something. Each action will help build on each other and you will feel accomplished. Feeling accomplished in the morning can lead to leaps and bounds of accomplishments by the end of the day.

Lastly, do something. Even if you don't know what to do, something is better than nothing. Oftentimes, when we do something, we will learn from that action, which will give us more clarity on what we actually want to do.

Again, Alan Watts has a video on YouTube called, *What If Money Was No Object?* This is a great short video, full of further insight.

Final thoughts

Enjoy the feeling of using your actions and love for the process. Whatever your goal or desire, by working on yourself, through meditation, journaling, exercising, practising gratitude, affirmations, or reading—really anything to make yourself feel better—the right actions will come into existence. If you were to only worry about feeling good, those will be the actions that are right for you. The question that I pose to you on this is, how much better could you feel? Always striving to feel better will lead to a lifetime of self-development. As you become better, you start attracting better. Work on actions that make you feel good and watch your world change.

Feel great, attract greatness!

CONCLUSION

Throughout this book, I have talked about many habits that worked for me to make me feel the best I have ever felt. Everything we do, regardless of our goal, if we dig deep enough, we are all striving to feel the pure feelings of love, happiness, abundance, appreciation, and bliss. I challenge you all to dive into some or all of the success habits, as they will help you tear down your self-limiting beliefs and help you create new powerful beliefs to help you realize your potential. An African proverb states, "When there is no enemy from within, the enemy outside can do you no harm." Remember, you have everything that you need already inside you; your job is to let it out.

For me, I always wanted to be great, but I didn't know how great I was. The moment that I realized that I am powerful, I am abundant, I am love, that is when the world moved mountains for me, and my world forever changed. I can feel the love and the abundance flow out of me; it's hard to describe, as it's a feeling, and until you feel it, you won't truly know it. I wish that all of you can realize your potential and feel how great you are, as once you feel it, then you become it. You are what you attract, so search for greatness and you will realize that you were always great.

I want to finish the conclusion off with one of my favourite quotations, said by Marianne Williamson:

"Our deepest fear is we are powerful beyond measure, it is our light not our darkness that most frightens us. You're playing small does not serve the world. There is nothing enlightened about shrinking so that other people won't feel insecure around you. We are all meant to shine as children do. It's not just in some of us; it's in everyone. As we let our own light shine, we unconsciously give other people permission to do the same. As we are liberated from our own fear, our presence automatically liberates others." (Marianne Williamson -1992)

As we discover how powerful we are, we are not only changing our lives, but we are changing the lives of the people around us. I initially wanted to be better for myself, and I enjoyed self-development, but when I realized that I needed to be the best person that I could be to show my kids what true love and happiness looks and feels like, that is when I took my learning to the next level. When I say learning, I really mean letting go of all the negative beliefs I had about myself to unleash my true potential. By intentionally tapping into my potential, everyone around me will get better as well. It will have a ripple effect, and who knows who I might inspire to live a more fulfilled life. Who knows who or what the outcome will be, but could you imagine a life of peace and no war, could you imagine a life where everyone is helping each other out instead of a world of greed and selfishness? Could you imagine a world of waking up with excitement and always feeling inspired to be your best every day? What does this look like? What will you do? How will you show up in life?

One of my favourite questions is, who am I? Remember, you are what you attract, so why not be great and attract greatness, as you could be the change the world needs to see?

ACKNOWLEDGMENTS

As I look at my life and as I finish this book, I feel extremely grateful. Where I am today is a direct reflection of the experiences and the people in my life. For all the good and for all the bad, I am thankful for everything and everyone as it has brought me to the point today to feel the best I have ever felt. I have came across some amazing people and some amazing colleagues and friends and for anyone who has ever met me, regardless of how much in contact we are, I can sincerely say, you have made an impact in my life and I will forever cherish our memories and interactions.

I first want to thank my parents, Dennis and Jeannie Boniface. Not only did they allow me to have a great childhood filled with sports and many trips to Florida, but they also helped pay for my University education, our wedding, and our first home. Most importantly over everything though, they helped paved the way for myself. They went through ups and downs and no matter what, they lived a life with hope and big dreams and showed me, with hard work and determination, you can achieve anything. The values that they instilled in me are priceless and I thank you for helping me create the belief system that I have today that leads to a life with no limits.

I secondly want to thank my best bud, my twin brother, Jeff Boniface. Some might say we are complete opposites, as true as that might be, we are also both one in the same. My whole life I have looked up to my bro, as he has always had the swag and the charisma to charm anyone. He is fearless and has accomplished what most people would never dream of doing. He has always challenged me to be a better version of myself and for that, I will be forever thankful!

Next, I want to thank my in-laws, Ray, Sharon and Mel Waddingham. They have been an amazing extension of our family and have provided me with an abundance of love, generosity, kindness and is always there to help out when in need. I feel so lucky and blessed to have you all in my life as you have all helped me become the man I am today. For that I am forever grateful!

Lastly, I want to thank my wife Carrie and kids Cali and Beau. There is no better feeling than pure love, and this is what you have given me. Every day, the love you all exude towards me, makes me realize that I am the luckiest guy in the world. I already have it all. To walk around knowing that my life is great as I have you all by my side is truly the best feeling. To Cali and Beau, every night when I check on you in your sleep and I see your pure innocence it makes me feel that love even more. I feel so proud to be your dad!

ABOUT THE AUTHOR

Derek Boniface loves his life. He epitomizes his message—*Feel Great, Attract Greatness*—he truly walks the talk.

Derek has spent the past fifteen years diving deep into self-development books and courses. He has done the leg work—challenging himself physically, mentally, and spiritually. He has discovered the truth and has a clear understanding of how to live your best life. Now, Derek wants to share with everyone what he has learned from all of his challenges in life and to give the discoveries that have taken him decades to understand all in one place—this book.

For the past twelve years, he has been the general manager of a GoodLife Fitness facility located in central Canada.

Feel Great, Attract Greatness: You Have What It Takes is his first book.

Derek lives in Smithville, Ontario, with his wife, Carrie, and their children, Cali and Beau.

CPSIA information can be obtained
at www.ICGtesting.com
Printed in the USA
BVHW030027210121
598258BV00004B/9/J